BLACK PANTHER VS. DEADPOOL

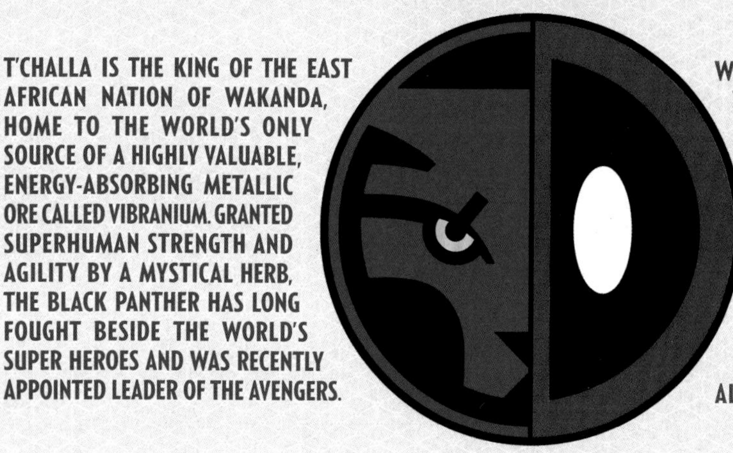

T'CHALLA IS THE KING OF THE EAST AFRICAN NATION OF WAKANDA, HOME TO THE WORLD'S ONLY SOURCE OF A HIGHLY VALUABLE, ENERGY-ABSORBING METALLIC ORE CALLED VIBRANIUM. GRANTED SUPERHUMAN STRENGTH AND AGILITY BY A MYSTICAL HERB, THE BLACK PANTHER HAS LONG FOUGHT BESIDE THE WORLD'S SUPER HEROES AND WAS RECENTLY APPOINTED LEADER OF THE AVENGERS.

WADE WILSON IS A MERCENARY WITH A HEALING FACTOR SO POWERFUL, HE'S UNKILLABLE. SO FAR, ANYWAY. THE ONLY THING MORE FEROCIOUS THAN HIS BODY'S ABILITY TO STITCH ITSELF BACK TOGETHER...IS THE RAGING CANCER THAT ALWAYS MANAGES TO GROW BACK WITH IT. HE'S BEEN A HERO AND A VILLAIN, BUT HE IS ALWAYS A GIANT PAIN IN THE @$$.

DANIEL KIBBLESMITH
WRITER

RICARDO LÓPEZ ORTIZ
ARTIST

FELIPE SOBREIRO
COLOR ARTIST

VC's JOE SABINO
LETTERER

RYAN BENJAMIN & RAIN BEREDO
COVER ARTISTS

SARAH BRUNSTAD
ASSOCIATE EDITOR

WIL MOSS
EDITOR

TOM BREVOORT
SENIOR EDITOR

BLACK PANTHER CREATED BY
STAN LEE & JACK KIRBY

DEADPOOL CREATED BY
ROB LIEFELD & FABIAN NICIEZA

COLLECTION EDITOR **MARK D. BEAZLEY**
ASSISTANT EDITOR **CAITLIN O'CONNELL**
ASSOCIATE MANAGING EDITOR **KATERI WOODY**
SENIOR EDITOR, SPECIAL PROJECTS **JENNIFER GRÜNWALD**
VP PRODUCTION & SPECIAL PROJECTS **JEFF YOUNGQUIST**
SVP PRINT, SALES & MARKETING **DAVID GABRIEL**

BOOK DESIGN **ADAM DEL RE**

EDITOR IN CHIEF **C.B. CEBULSKI**
CHIEF CREATIVE OFFICER **JOE QUESADA**
PRESIDENT **DAN BUCKLEY**
EXECUTIVE PRODUCER **ALAN FINE**

BLACK PANTHER VS. DEADPOOL. Contains material originally published in magazine form as BLACK PANTHER VS. DEADPOOL #1-5. First printing 2019. ISBN 978-1-302-91549-0. Published by MARVEL WORLDWIDE, INC., a subsidiary of MARVEL ENTERTAINMENT, LLC. OFFICE OF PUBLICATION: 135 West 50th Street, New York, NY 10020. **Printed in Canada**. DAN BUCKLEY, President, Marvel Entertainment; JOHN NEE, Publisher; JOE QUESADA, Chief Creative Officer; TOM BREVOORT, SVP of Publishing; DAVID BOGART, SVP of Business Affairs & Operations, Publishing & Partnership; DAVID GABRIEL, SVP of Sales & Marketing, Publishing; JEFF YOUNGQUIST, VP of Production & Special Projects; DAN CARR, Executive Director of Publishing Technology; ALEX MORALES, Director of Publishing Operations; DAN EDINGTON, Managing Editor; SUSAN CRESPI, Production Manager; STAN LEE, Chairman Emeritus. For information regarding advertising in Marvel Comics or on Marvel.com, please contact Vit DeBellis, Custom Solutions & Integrated Advertising Manager, at vdebellis@marvel.com. For Marvel subscription inquiries, please call 888-511-5480. **Manufactured between 1/25/2019 and 2/26/2019 by SOLISCO PRINTERS, SCOTT, QC, CANADA.**

10 9 8 7 6 5 4 3 2 1

1

HOW DO YOU BECOME A KING?

T'CHALLA,
SON OF T'CHAKA, KING AND PROTECTOR OF WAKANDA, AND THE LEGENDARY HERO KNOWN AS THE
BLACK PANTHER

I WAS NOT *BORN* A KING. A *PRINCE*, YES.
FATHER KING
DID I BECOME A KING THE MOMENT MY FATHER DIED?

I DID NOT *FEEL* DIFFERENT. I DID NOT FEEL *READY.*
AND YET IN THAT MOMENT, I *MUST* HAVE BEEN KING. FOR THE ALTERNATIVE IS *UNACCEPTABLE* TO ME.

THAT EVEN FOR ONE MOMENT, *WAKANDA HAD NO KING.*
KNOCK
KNOCK

ARE YOU READY, BROTHER?
YES?
FOR GENERATIONS, OUR NATION SURVIVED BY CLOSING OURSELVES OFF. WHEN THE WOULD-BE COLONIZERS CAME TO OUR DOORSTEP BEARING *"GIFTS,"* WE TOOK NOTHING AND GAVE NOTHING. *NOT ONE INCH.*
BUT THAT WAS THE WAKANDA OF OLD. AND IN THIS *BRAVE NEW WORLD*

...I'M NOT SURE I CAN CONTROL WHAT HAPPENS NEXT.
BLACK PANTHER VS. DEADPOOL
PART ONE: A SMALL MISUNDERSTANDING

UBUSUKU BOKUFA. WAKANDA'S "NIGHT OF THE DEAD," WHEN THE VEIL BETWEEN THE WORLDS OF LIFE AND DEATH IS AT ITS THINNEST AND OUR ANCESTORS WALK BESIDE US.
FOR MANY WAKANDANS, THIS IS NOT A METAPHOR.

MY SISTER, SHURI, IS A BELIEVER. AFTER ALL, SHE HERSELF CROSSED OVER AND RETURNED TO US.
BROTHER, EVEN SMILING YOU APPEAR TROUBLED.

WHAT CAN I SAY? YOU INHERITED FATHER'S WISDOM. I INHERITED HIS WORRY.
I SHOULD BE IN THE LAB. WE ARE ON THE VERGE OF A DISCOVERY THAT COULD SAVE COUNTLESS WAKANDAN LIVES.

WAKANDANS ALSO NEED TO SEE THEIR KING. THE "STAR CELLS" WILL BE THERE WHEN YOU RETURN.
BUT WHAT DO WE ENCOURAGE ON THIS NIGHT? A COUNTRY IS ITS CHILDREN, AND WE TEACH OURS TO WORSHIP DEATH AND DRESS AS MONSTERS.
NOT ALL OF THEM, BROTHER.

SOME DRESS AS HEROES.

HELLO. ARE YOU THE BLACK PANTHER?
...YES.
THAT IS WONDERFUL. I AM ALSO THE BLACK PANTHER.

HERE. CANDY FROM AMERICA.
IT IS ESSENTIALLY A SMALL AMOUNT OF POISON. BUT THE BLACK PANTHER IS STRONG.

BWWAAAAAH!
I DON'T-- I'M SORRY! WHY DOES SHE CRY? DID I FRIGHTEN HER?
NO, MY KING. SHE IS GRATEFUL FOR YOUR GIFT.

SHE CRIES BECAUSE SHE HAS NOTHING TO GIVE YOU IN RETURN.

DO NOT CRY, LITTLE PANTHER. YOU HAVE GIVEN ME EVERYTHING.
OKAY, WE GET IT! T'CHALLA IS A GOOD KING! CAN WE PLEASE GET TO THE EXCITING STUFF?

FINALLY!
WADE WILSON.
THE SELF-REGENERATIN', SWORD-SLINGIN', GUN-TOTIN', JOKE-SPOUTIN' MERCENARY KNOWN AS
DEADPOOL
SCARY RICHARD'S BUSY BURG!
HAVE YOU GUYS READ THIS?! THIS IS EXACTLY WHAT I'M ALWAYS SAYING!

AAAAHH!
IF WE'RE GONNA SURVIVE AS A SOCIETY, WE ALL GOTTA WORK TOGETHER. LIKE THESE LITTLE ANIMALS IN HATS!
THERE'S A BAKER AND A FRIENDLY NEIGHBORHOOD MAILMAN AND-- LOOK! THE POLICE CHIEF IS A KITTY!

SEE, IT'S ALL ABOUT CIVIC RESPONSIBILITY!
I SHOULD PROBABLY TRY TO FOCUS.
GIVE IT UP, DEADPOOL!

THE WRECKER.
WRECKS THINGS.
THOSE PRIVATE SCHOOL BRATS ARE GONNA FETCH ME A KING'S RANSOM! THEN ME AND MY MAGIC CROWBAR ARE GONNA POUND YOU INTO DEAD-MEAT!
YIKES. WAS THAT SUPPOSED TO BE A PUN?

NO WONDER THE WRECKER'S NOT IN ANY OF THE MOVIES.
WELL IF IT ISN'T MY FAVORITE FRIENDLY NEIGHBORHOOD MAILMAN, WILLIE LUMPKIN!
LOOKS LIKE JUST BILLS TODAY, DORIS!
WELL, ALL NEWS IS GOOD NEWS IF IT COMES FROM YOU, WILLIE.

SAY...IS THAT SCHOOL BUS DRIVING ON THE SIDEWALK?

OKAY, TIMMY, KEEP THOSE HANDS AT TEN AND TWO LIKE I SHOWED YOU. MISTER POOL'S GOTTA GO KICK SOME @$$.
MY NAME'S NOT TIMMY, IT'S LIN-MANUEL BARACK KHALEESI.

SIGH OF COURSE IT IS.
FWUMP!

THAT'S WHAT I GET FOR RESCUING A BUSLOAD OF KIDS IN BROOKLYN.
NOW WHERE DID I PUT--
?
PEOPLE JUST LOVE TO MAKE FUN OF THE POUCHES. "HEY DEADPOOL, THE '90s CALLED. THEY WANT THEIR POUCHES BACK." ETC., ETC.
BUT I GOT EVERYTHING IN THESE BABIES.

--AHA!
LIKE, SAY, A THERMITE GRENADE CAPABLE OF BURNING THROUGH AN INDUSTRIAL STEEL CHAIN.

HISSS
OKAY, SEXY WRECKSY, TODAY'S YOUR LUCKY DAY, BECAUSE I'VE BEEN WAITING YEARS TO BE ABLE TO QUOTE THIS CATCHPHRASE LEGALLY...

VOOOOM!
"LET'S GET DANGEROUS!"

SMACK!
OOMPH.

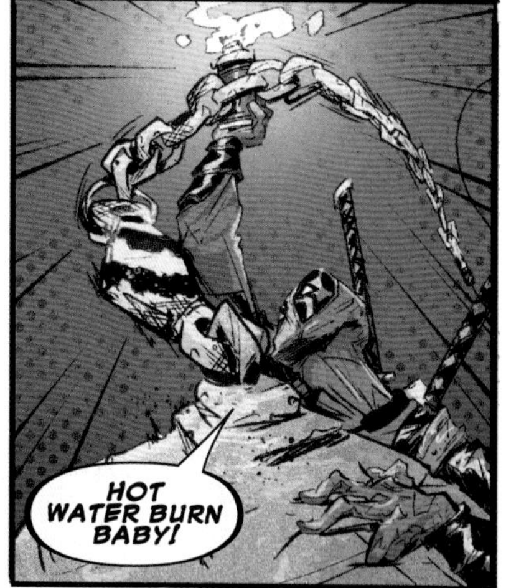
HOT WATER BURN BABY!

HISSS!
CRINK!

TA-DA!
KERKRUNCH!
NOOO!

IRRRRRT!

ERRF! MY CROW--
OH NO YOU DON'T!
YOU KNOW, I HAVE NEVER UNDERSTOOD WHY SOMEONE DOESN'T JUST TAKE THIS STUPID THING AWAY FROM YOU.

OOH--ILL-DEFINED ENCHANTED METAL!
I'M SURE THIS WON'T COME UP AGAIN LATER!
UH, MISTER POOL?

TIMMY! MY MAN! YOU REALLY CAME THROUGH BACK THERE!
WE STOPPED THE BAD GUY AND EVERYONE'S OKAY! IT'S LIKE I SAID--CIVIC RESPONSIBILITY.
THANKS, MISTER POOL, BUT...

...NOT EVERYONE'S OKAY.
HELP! GET HELP!
NO!
DORIS? MY MOUTH TASTES LIKE PENNIES.

NOT THE FRIENDLY NEIGHBORHOOD MAILMAN!
HE'S STABLE FOR NOW, BUT IT'S NOT LOOKING GOOD, MISTER--
--SORRY, HOW ARE YOU RELATED TO THE PATIENT AGAIN?

I'M HIS SON, DEADPOOL.
DEADPOOL LUMPKIN.
WELL, MISTER LUMPKIN, IT'S NOT LOOKING GREAT. THE SHRAPNEL INCHES CLOSER TO YOUR FATHER'S HEART EVERY TIME HE BREATHES.

PLEASE, DOC! AN INNOCENT PERSON IS HURT, AND FOR THE FIRST TIME (SINCE I LEARNED ABOUT CIVIC RESPONSIBILITY) IT'S MY FAULT! THERE MUST BE SOMETHING I CAN DO!
WELL, THERE IS AN EXPERIMENTAL TREATMENT OUT THERE. TONY STARK PIONEERED SOMETHING SIMILAR ONE OF THE TIMES HE CURED HIMSELF FROM BEING IRON MAN.

VIBRANIUM THERAPY.
AN INCH-LONG PIECE TUNED TO THE RIGHT RESONANCE COULD EXPEL THE FOREIGN SUBSTANCES NEAR HIS HEART.
BUT OF COURSE, GETTING VIBRANIUM IS NEXT TO IMPOSSI--

IS THAT ALL?! ONE TEENSY-WEENSY PIECE OF VIBRANIUM?!
THAT'S NO PROBLEM! I TOTALLY KNOW A GUY! WE'RE BOTH BASICALLY AVENGERS!

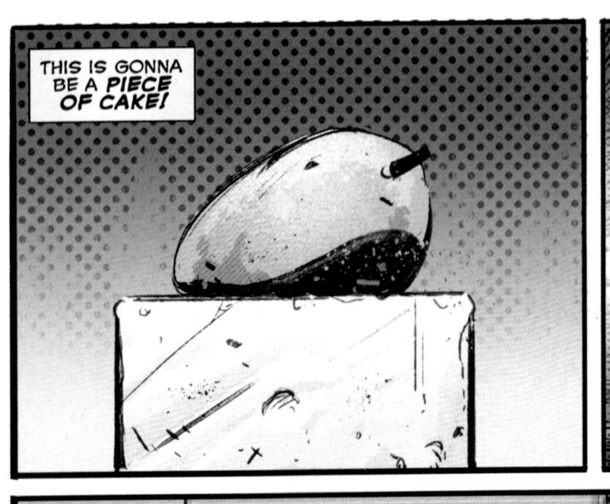
THIS IS GONNA BE A PIECE OF CAKE!

VERSSH!
(I'M JUST KIDDING. I CAN SMELL A DEADPOOL VS. WHOEVER COMIN' A MILE AWAY.)

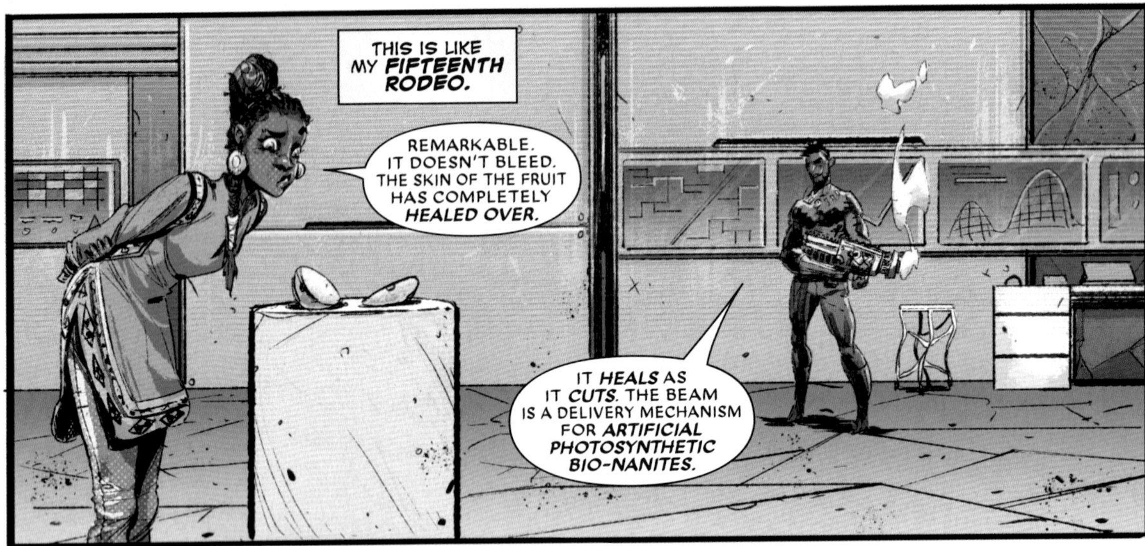
THIS IS LIKE MY FIFTEENTH RODEO.
REMARKABLE. IT DOESN'T BLEED. THE SKIN OF THE FRUIT HAS COMPLETELY HEALED OVER.
IT HEALS AS IT CUTS. THE BEAM IS A DELIVERY MECHANISM FOR ARTIFICIAL PHOTOSYNTHETIC BIO-NANITES.

THE "STAR CELLS."
ARTIFICIAL UNIVERSAL-DONOR STEM CELLS. SURGERY WITHOUT BLEEDING OR INFECTION.
IF I CAN MINIATURIZE THIS TECH INTO A SCALPEL, WE COULD TRANSFORM FIELD MEDICINE, SAVING THOUSANDS WOUNDED IN WAR OR BY LAND MINES.
YOU WISH TO END WAR, SO YOU BUILT A GUN.
...FOR TESTING PURPOSES, A LARGER PROTOTYPE WAS EASIER TO--
I AM JUST TEASING, T'CHALLA. GOD, YOU'RE SUCH A BOY.
YOUR MAJESTY!

WHAT IS IT, OKOYE?
FORGIVE MY INTRUSION, SIRE. WE HAVE A, UH, SITUATION.
NO. NOT HIM.

ANYONE BUT HIM.
HAKUNA MATATA, YOUR MAJESTY!

MY GOD. THAT IS THE WORST THING HE COULD HAVE SAID.
GIVE HIM TIME.

WE FOUND HIM IN THE ROYAL GARDENS. HE SOMEHOW SLIPPED THROUGH OUR DEFENSES.
HOW IS THAT POSSIBLE?

OOH! I CAN FIELD THAT ONE!

OKAY, ACCORDING TO THIS HERE CONSERVATION EXCHANGE AGREEMENT, THESE ELEPHANTS ARE GOING BACK TO WAKANDA.
MOOOOO!
BRONX ZOO
TRANSFER LIST

MOO!

WAIT, DO YOU THINK ELEPHANTS MOO?
I THINK IT'S 4:45 ON A FRIDAY. GET 'EM ON THE TRUCK.

THEN THERE WAS A NINETEEN-HOUR FLIGHT, AND A NUMBER OF MATING ATTEMPTS THAT I DID NOT RECIPROCATE, AND--
ENOUGH!

YOU ARE HERE. SO, WHAT DO YOU WANT?

WHAT? OH! JUST A LITTLE PIECE OF VIBRANIUM.
ABOUT YEA BIG.

SO...THE SIZE OF A BULLET.

AW, C'MON, CHALLY! IT AIN'T LIKE THAT!
BESIDES, WE BOTH KNOW HOW THIS IS GONNA GO DOWN.
ENLIGHTEN ME.
OH, LIKE YOU DON'T KNOW. THESE SUPER HERO DUSTUPS HAVE A RHYTHM TO THEM!

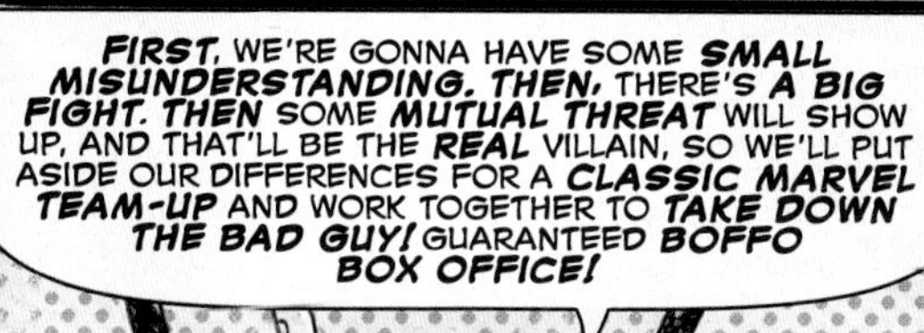
FIRST, WE'RE GONNA HAVE SOME SMALL MISUNDERSTANDING. THEN, THERE'S A BIG FIGHT. THEN SOME MUTUAL THREAT WILL SHOW UP, AND THAT'LL BE THE REAL VILLAIN, SO WE'LL PUT ASIDE OUR DIFFERENCES FOR A CLASSIC MARVEL TEAM-UP AND WORK TOGETHER TO TAKE DOWN THE BAD GUY! GUARANTEED BOFFO BOX OFFICE!

SO WHADDYA SAY WE SKIP ALL THAT, CUT TO THE CHASE, AND YOU GIVE ME AN INCH OF VIBRANIUM SO I CAN GET BACK IN MY SEXY ELEPHANT COSTUME AND GET OUTTA YOUR HAIR?

NOT ONE INCH.
NO.

NO?!
I KNOW WHO YOU ARE, WADE WILSON. CAPTAIN AMERICA'S BAFFLING RESPECT FOR YOU BOUGHT YOU THESE PRECIOUS SECONDS OF MY TIME.

BUT THE BLACK PANTHER DOES NOT JUDGE THE MAN. HE SEES THE SOUL.
YOU TELL YOURSELF YOU ARE A HERO. BUT I SEE A MURDERER AND A THIEF, ASKING FOR A PIECE OF MY COUNTRY'S VERY HEART.

EITHER YOU ARE PLANNING SOME GREAT CATASTROPHE OR IT IS ALREADY DONE.
UNLESS I AM WRONG?
I... I...

I DON'T HAVE TO EXPLAIN MYSELF TO YOU! TO ANY OF YOU!
YOU KNOW WHAT? FINE. I LET IT SLIDE WHEN THEY GAVE YOU TOP BILLING ON THIS BOOK. BUT NOW I GUESS WE'RE DOING THIS THE HARD WAY. TIME FOR THE...
...SMALL MISUNDERSTANDING!
URK!
THAT--
GRAB
--IS THE STUPIDEST THING YOU HAVE EVER DONE.
WHAM!

GUARDS! LEAVE US. I WILL NOT HAVE THIS CRIMINAL SPILLING WAKANDAN BLOOD.
SHURI, DO YOU WISH TO--
YES.

BADLY.

AAAAAH! WHAT THE HELL?!
I'M BEING ATTACKED BY BIRDS! JUST LIKE IN THAT CLASSIC HORROR MOVIE THE GUARDIANS OF GA'HOOLE!

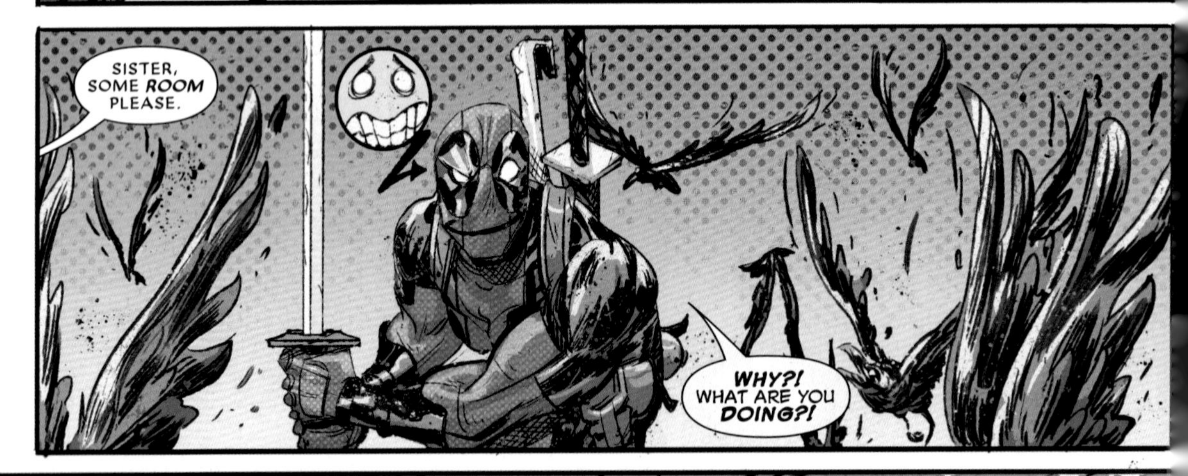
SISTER, SOME ROOM PLEASE.
WHY?! WHAT ARE YOU DOING?!

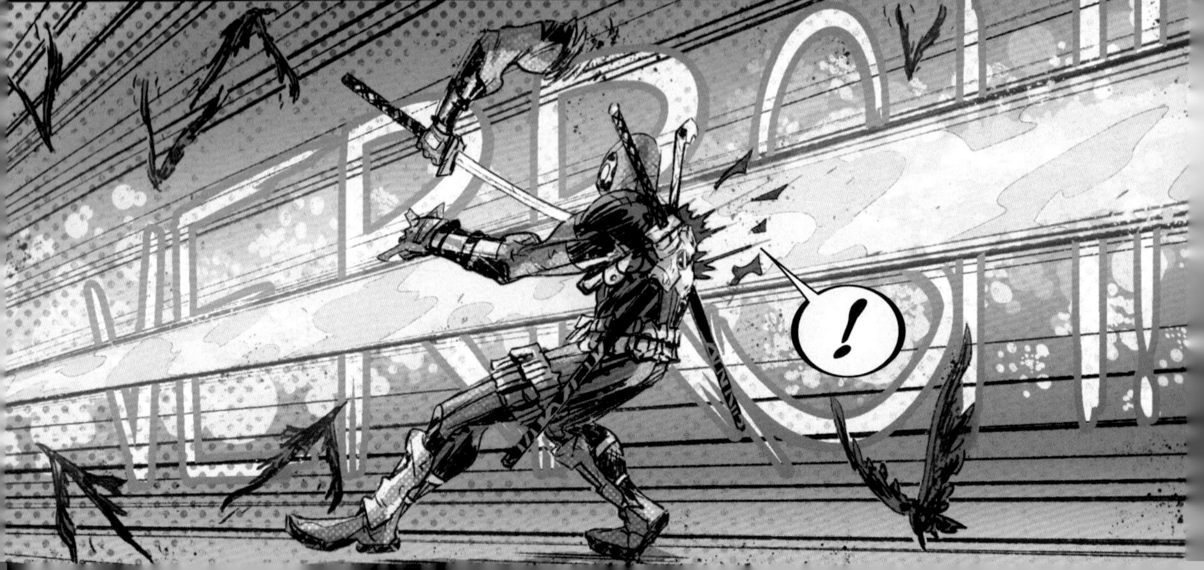
!

DISARMING YOU.

OH, SO NOW YOU HAVE A SENSE OF HUMOR?!
FASCINATING.

WHAT'S FASCINATING?! WHY ISN'T MY ARM GROWING BACK? WHY DO I FEEL ALL TINGLY?!
AND NOT IN THE GOOD WAY!
BROTHER, IT APPEARS THE STAR CELLS ARE NEUTRALIZING HIS HEALING FACTOR WHERE THEY MADE CONTACT.

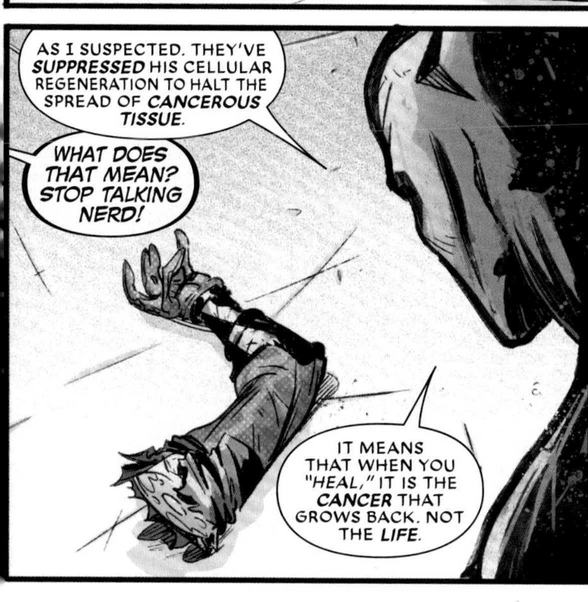
AS I SUSPECTED. THEY'VE SUPPRESSED HIS CELLULAR REGENERATION TO HALT THE SPREAD OF CANCEROUS TISSUE.
WHAT DOES THAT MEAN? STOP TALKING NERD!
IT MEANS THAT WHEN YOU "HEAL," IT IS THE CANCER THAT GROWS BACK. NOT THE LIFE.

YOU NEVER HAD A HEALING FACTOR. YOU HAVE A DYING FACTOR.

...FINE! I DON'T NEED YOU RICH SNOBS! I'LL GET MY OWN VIBRANIUM! I'LL STEAL ULTRON'S PELVIS OR SOMETHING!
JUST GIVE ME BACK MY ARM!

OOF!
THAT IS TWICE THAT YOU HAVE DRAWN A WEAPON AGAINST ME IN MY HOME!

STAY. DOWN!

YOU KNOW, *COUGH* YOU'RE A LOT NICER IN THE MOVIE.

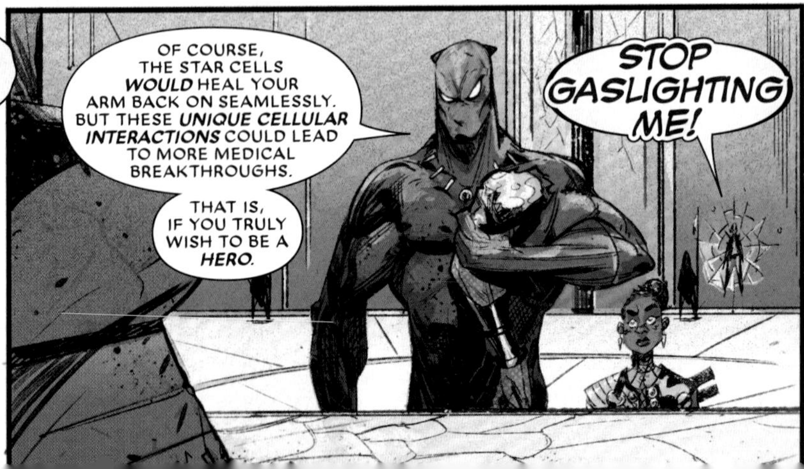
OF COURSE, THE STAR CELLS WOULD HEAL YOUR ARM BACK ON SEAMLESSLY. BUT THESE UNIQUE CELLULAR INTERACTIONS COULD LEAD TO MORE MEDICAL BREAKTHROUGHS.
THAT IS, IF YOU TRULY WISH TO BE A HERO.
STOP GASLIGHTING ME!

HMM. THIS ENERGY SIGNATURE...YOU HAVE A TELEPORTATION DEVICE ON YOUR PERSON?
SO WHAT? I GOT EVERYTHING IN THESE POUCHES! DIDN'T YOU READ THE PART WITH THE WRECKER?!
WHAT IS ITS RANGE?
HOW THE $#&% SHOULD I KNOW?! I STOPPED USING THAT THING IN LIKE 2012.

I'M HACKING IT.
WADE WILSON-- THE VERY ESSENCE OF CREATION HAS DEEMED YOU A CANCER THAT MUST NOT SPREAD BACK INTO OUR UNIVERSE.
YOU'RE WHAT?!
LEAVE MY COUNTRY AND MY SIGHT.

"WE'LL MAIL YOU THE ARM."
NO NO NO NO NO NO NOOO!

THUMPH!
OKAY, YEAH. DEFINITELY LANDED ON MY SWORD.

OKAY, T'CHALLA. IF THAT'S HOW YOU WANNA PLAY IT, SO BE IT.
YOU WANNA KNOW HOW SOMEBODY GETS TO BE KING? BECAUSE I KNOW HOW YOU BECOME A KING.

SHLICK

YOU CUT THE HEAD OFF A KING.

AVENGERS...
DISASSEMBLE HIM!
(THIS TOTALLY HAPPENS IN THIS ISSUE, BTW.)

BLAM!

AZANIA, JUST OFF THE WAKANDAN BORDER...
KILLER SHOT, DURNIS!
THANK YOU, CLEMSON, MY DEAR TWIN BROTHER. THERE'S NO RUSH LIKE THE LIFE-OR-DEATH STRUGGLE OF SHOOTING AN ANIMAL THAT DOESN'T KNOW YOU EXIST.

...LEGAL GRAY AREA FOR BIG-GAME HUNTERS.
ESPECIALLY APEX PREDATORS LIKE THE DEADLY AFRICAN ZEBRA.

YOU SAID IT, BRO. I JUST WISH DAD WAS HERE TO SEE HOW ALPHA WE ARE.
BLEHHH.

YOU KNOW IT, BROSEPH. THEN WE'D GET THOSE SWEET, SWEET HUGS FOR SURE.
EXCUSE ME, YOU FINE YOUNG GENTLEMEN!
HUH?

I'D LIKE TO MAKE YOU AN OFFER YOU CAN'T REFUSE!
BLACK PANTHER VS. DEADPOOL
PART TWO: A BIG FIGHT!

HIS CAN'T BE RIGHT.
WADE WILSON A.K.A. DEADPOOL
CANADIAN
MUTANT-ADJACENT
ABILITIES: RAPID SELF-REGENERATIVE PROPERTIES, COMBAT EXPERT.
WEAKNESSES: "CHIMICHANGAS" (UNKNOWN SUBSTANCE)

I WAS CORRECT IN MY ASSESSMENT. DEADPOOL'S *REGENERATION* ABILITIES ARE A BY-PRODUCT OF HIS HYPERMUTATED *CANCER*.
IT'S WHY HE ONLY GROWS BACK *DISFIGURED TISSUE*. AT THIS POINT, WADE WILSON MIGHT LITERALLY BE ONE GIANT *TUMOR*.

BUT WHEN WILSON'S SELF-REPLICATING CELLS INTERACT WITH THE *STAR CELLS* THAT SHURI AND I INVENTED--OUR ARTIFICIAL *UNIVERSAL HEALING* MICROBES--THEY DON'T JUST STOP THE SPREAD OF HIS CANCER. THEY *FREEZE DEGENERATION* COMPLETELY.
IF MY ANALYSIS IS CORRECT, THEN THE UNTHINKABLE HAS OCCURRED.

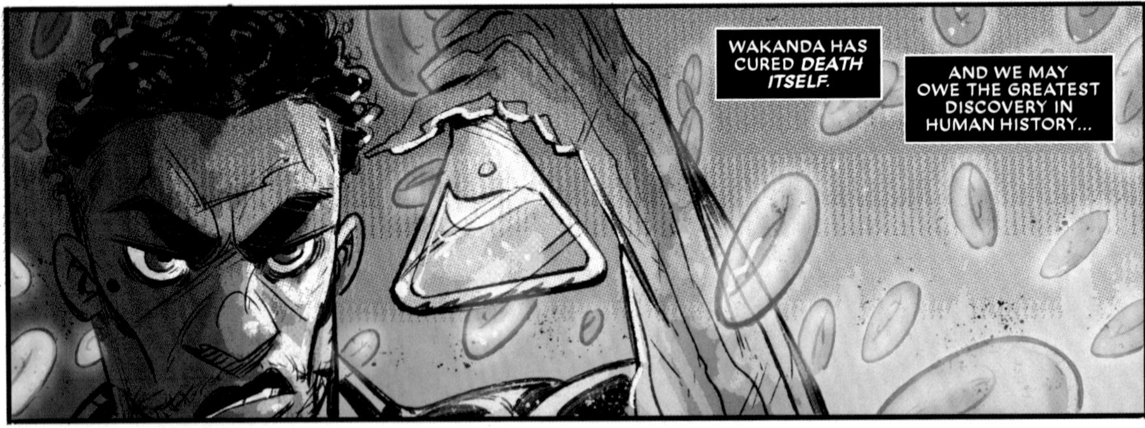
WAKANDA HAS CURED *DEATH ITSELF*.
AND WE MAY OWE THE GREATEST DISCOVERY IN HUMAN HISTORY...

...TO *DEADPOOL*.
I--I SHOULD CLEAR MY HEAD...

...BEFORE I TOO DO SOMETHING UNTHINKABLE.
DEADPOOL?! I'M YOUR BIGGEST FAN! I HAVE YOUR BASEBALL CAP!
THANKS FOR READING MY COMICS, KID.
YOU'RE IN COMICS?
BUP BUP! QUIET TIME.

I SAID I WANTED TO SPEAK TO THE GENTLEMEN.
<AFTERNOON! BEAUTIFUL COUNTRY YOU HAVE HERE.>
<YOU SPEAK AZANIAN?>
<NO, BUT I'M FLUENT IN TRANSLATED WORD BALLOON.>

<SO WHAT'S THE BUSINESS MODEL HERE? HELPING FOREIGN HUNTERS SHOOT BELOVED ANIMALS FOR FUN AND PROFIT?>
<ARE YOU JOKING? IT BREAKS OUR HEARTS TO SEE THESE CREATURES KILLED SO SOME AMERICAN BABY-MAN CAN TAKE A SELFIE.>

<BUT WHAT ELSE CAN WE DO? THERE ARE NO CODING JOBS HERE. NO CALL CENTERS.>
<YOUR "GLOBAL ECONOMY" LEAVES US BEHIND...>

<...SO WE MAKE OUR LIVING ANY WAY WE KNOW HOW.>

‹HARD RELATE. OKAY, DO YOU TAKE SHADOWY BLACK-MARKET CRYPTOCURRENCIES?›
‹OBVIOUSLY.›
‹SUPER. HOW ABOUT I TRANSFER YOU ENOUGH UNTRACEABLE CASH THAT YOU NEVER HAVE TO BABYSIT SOME PASTY DEATH-TOURIST EVER AGAIN? AND IN EXCHANGE...›

YOU GIMME ONE OF 'DEM JEEPS.
WHAT?! THERE'S FIVE OF US! HOW WILL WE CARRY ALL OUR DEAD ANIMALS HOME?

NOT MY PROB. I GOTTA GO BACK TO WAKANDA AND GET MY ARM. PLUS SOME VIBRANIUM FOR MY "EMOTIONAL DISTRESS."
AND MY TELEPORTER IS ON THE FRITZ SINCE HIS MAJESTY KING T'JERKA HACKED IT AND DUMPED ME ON A MOUNTAIN.
BZZT!!

YOU'RE NOT TAKING OUR RIDE, BRO. I'M NOT LEAVING THE COUNTRY OF AFRICA WITHOUT MY TROPHIES.
SIGH YOU KNOW, I THINK I'M STARTING TO SEE THE APPEAL.
OF WHAT, HUNTING?
NAW, DOGG.

KTHUNK!

I LOVE HUNTING.
AIEEEE!!!

I MEAN TAKING TROPHIES.

T'CHALLA SAID THIS BLUE STUFF WAS SOME KIND OF UNIVERSAL HEALING SOLVENT. SO THIS HANDY SEVERED ARM SHOULD STICK RIGHT ON, NO PROBLEM!
GET IT? "HANDY"?
BLEHHHHH!!

BLEHHHH!
OH CRAP. YOU'RE NOT DEAD.

CURSE MY BIG, MUSHY HEART.
BLEH?

OKAY, FELLA--CLOSE YOUR EYES AND COUNT TO THREE.

"YOU'RE GOIN' TO A BETTER PLACE."
HE WAS ALWAYS YOUR FAVORITE.

I DO NOT HAVE "FAVORITES."
I UNDERSTAND HE WAS YOUR GRANDFATHER'S FAVORITE TOO.

T'CHAKA SAID AZZURI ALWAYS PULLED HIS PUNCHES WITH THAT ONE.
RAMONDA. MY MOTHER IN ALL BUT BIRTH.

THE CAPTAIN PULLS HIS PUNCHES TOO.
PUNFF!

HONOR IS OUR GREATEST STRENGTH. UNTIL IT IS NOT.
WHAT WORRIES ME...

"...ARE THE MEN WITHOUT HONOR."
DRAMATIC MUSIC!

‹THERE'S RUMORS OF A SMUGGLER'S ROUTE--A BLIND SPOT IN WAKANDA'S DEFENSES. TUNNELS THAT LEAD BENEATH THE ROYAL PALACE ITSELF.›
‹OF COURSE, NO ONE HAS EVER COME BACK.›

DRAMAAATIC MUUUSIC!

YOU TELL YOURSELF YOU ARE A HERO. BUT I SEE A MURDERER AND A THIEF.

DRAAAMAAATIC MUUUSIC!!!

LUMPKINNNNNN!!!
GOTTA HAND IT TO YOU, DEADPOOL. YOU'RE AN EVEN BIGGER WRECKER THAN ME.

DRAAAMAAATIC MUUUSIC!!!
BLEHHH!
QUIET, YOU.
VROOOM!

MOTHER, I...I DON'T LIKE YOU SEEING ME LIKE THIS.
I RAISED YOU, T'CHALLA. I AM WELL AWARE OF YOUR TEMPER.
PFFT!
CAMOUFLAGED MEMORY MOLECULES. THE IRON MAN FILTRATION SYSTEM WELCOMES THEM IN AS PURE OXYGEN.

UNTIL THEY BEGIN TO VIBRATE. VERY LOUDLY, I'M TOLD. LIKE A BULLET TRAIN PASSING BETWEEN YOUR SINUSES.
IF YOU ARE EMBARRASSED, THEN WHY AM I HERE?
I MUST ASK YOU A DIFFICULT QUESTION. AND TIME MAY BE SHORT. MOTHER...

...AM I THE GREATEST OF THE BLACK PANTHERS?
"THE MADDER THE HULK GETS, THE STRONGER THE HULK GETS." BUT EVEN A HULK IS MOSTLY WATER.

AIM FOR SOMETHING SOFT AND WET--

MY SON.

--AND LET ELECTRICITY WORK HER WONDERS.
IT IS NOT LIKE YOU TO SEEK VALIDATION.
HIS AMYGDALA RESPONDS BY OVERLOADING THE CONTRACTING MUSCLES, AND JUST LIKE THAT?

STRENGTH BECOMES WEAKNESS.
THAT'S THE THEORY, ANYWAY. I HOPE NEVER TO FIND OUT.
KER-THOOMP

END SIMULATION.
KIMOYO TECH HARD-LIGHT PROJECTOR. STILL CHEAPER THAN A GYM MEMBERSHIP.

IT IS NOT A QUESTION OF VANITY, MOTHER, BUT OF NECESSITY.
I HAVE NO HEIR. SHURI HAS NO HEIR. YET THERE MUST ALWAYS BE A BLACK PANTHER.
IF I AM TRULY THE STRONGEST PROTECTOR WAKANDA HAS EVER KNOWN...IF I FOUND A WAY TO REMAIN SO...WOULD IT NOT BE LOGICAL FOR ME TO...

MOTHER. I FEAR I AM ON THE VERGE OF COMMITTING A GREAT SIN.

FWEEEE
T'CHALLA? WHAT IS THIS?
I APOLOGIZE, MOTHER. TIME WAS SHORTER THAN I THOUGHT.
GET DOWN.
FWEEEEEEEE

BOOM
HEY, T'CHALLA!
WHAT'S BLACK AND WHITE AND RED ALL OVER?!
BLEHHH!

WHAM!
HOW DARE YOU?!

I KNEW YOU WERE STUPID ENOUGH TO RETURN, BUT I'D HOPED MY GUARDS WOULD SPARE ME THE GUILT OF PERSONALLY ENDING YOU.
TAKEN OUT BY RANDOM GUARDS? IN MY OWN CROSSOVER?! NO WAY, B.P.-- THIS IS FATE.
FIRST THE SMALL MISUNDERSTANDING...

THEN THE BIG FIGHT!
KASHANG!

YOU'RE PROBABLY WONDERING ABOUT MY NEW PAL HERE, RIGHT?
THOSE STAR CELLS 'A YOURS REALLY DO WORK WONDERS!
BLEHHH.

DOESN'T MATTER--
KTUNG!
--I CAN STILL BEAT YOU WITH ONE HAND TIED BEHIND YOUR BACK!

NOT SO CHATTY THIS TIME! PANTHER GOT YOUR TONGUE?
I AM CONCENTRATING.
ON WHAT? GETTING YER @$$ BEAT?
NO, ON--
KCHUNK!

NO, ON GETTING MY MOTHER TO SAFETY.

--TO SAFETY. END SIMULATION.
WHAT IN THE NAME OF DEAN STOCKWELL??

PUNCH!!!
ERK!

CHEAP SHOT, BRO!
YOU KNOW, WE COULDA SKIPPED THIS WHOLE GRATUITOUS FIGHT SCENE IF YOU'D JUST BELIEVED ME ABOUT THE VIBRANIUM!
BELIEVED YOU?!

YOU BELIEVE IN NOTHING!
SWIPE!

YOU HAVE NO COUNTRY! YOU HAVE NO FAMILY!
NOW THAT'S NOT STRICTLY-- OOF!

NO LEGACY TO UPHOLD! NO GODS!

YOU DON'T EVEN CARRY THE WEIGHT OF YOUR OWN DEATH!
KERASSH

THERE IS NO *YOU* TO *BELIEVE!*

BLEHHHH!!!
CHOMP!

AND NOW YOU *MUTILATE* THIS ANIMAL?!
FOR WHAT, A *JOKE?* I SHOULD FINISH *DISMEMBERING* YOU AND FIRE THE PIECES INTO *SPACE*.
»WHEEZE« I KEEP *TELLIN'* YOU, *B.P.*, IT AIN'T *LIKE* THAT.
I'M NOT LIKE THAT. WELL, AT LEAST *THIS* TIME.

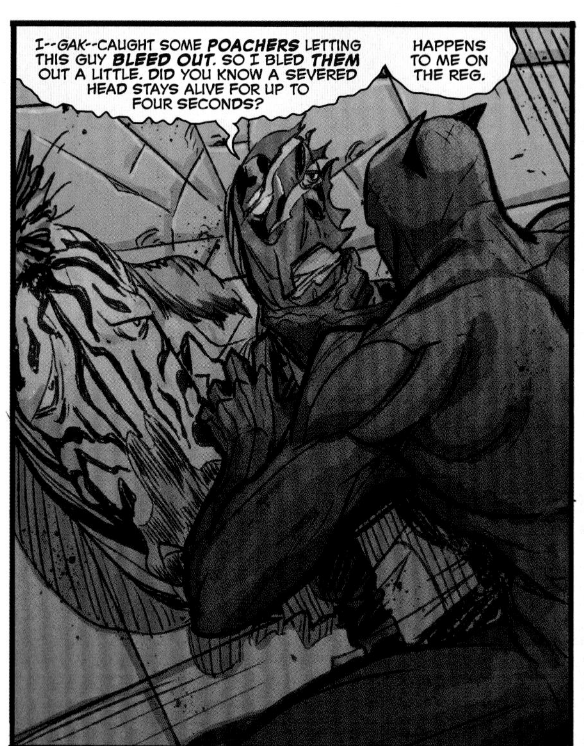
I--GAK--CAUGHT SOME POACHERS LETTING THIS GUY BLEED OUT. SO I BLED THEM OUT A LITTLE. DID YOU KNOW A SEVERED HEAD STAYS ALIVE FOR UP TO FOUR SECONDS?
HAPPENS TO ME ON THE REG.

GAAAASP

GET UP.

WAIT, IS THAT IT? ARE WE DONE VERSUS-ING ALREADY?

I WILL RETRIEVE YOUR ARM FROM MY LAB, AND YOU WILL LEAVE WAKANDA FOREVER.
"WAKANDA FOREVER"? HEY, THAT'S CATCHY.
BUT LOOK, I THINK YOU'RE FORGETTING ABOUT MY WHOLE INCITING INCIDENT? I'M NOT GOING ANYWHERE WITHOUT THAT INCH-LONG PIECE OF VIBRANIUM.

THE FACT THAT I AM ALLOWING YOU TO LEAVE IN ONE PIECE IS A BLESSING.
OH YEAH? THEN WHAT HAPPENS TO MY PAL SPOT HERE?
"SPOT"?

"STRIPEY" SEEMED TOO OBVIOUS.
⌯SIGH⌯ I WILL THINK OF SOMETHING.

BWOOP!

OKOYE.
MY KING. WE HAVE ANOTHER SITUATION.
YES, OUR "SITUATION" IS RIGHT HERE. I HAVE DEALT WITH HIM. AGAIN.
HIYEEEE!

I TAKE FULL RESPONSIBILITY FOR HIS INFILTRATION, SIRE. BUT THIS TIME DEADPOOL IS NOT THE CRISIS.
REALLY? THAT DOESN'T SOUND LIKE ME.
A FEW MINUTES AGO, A PRIVATE PLANE TOOK OFF FROM AZANIA TOWARD WAKANDAN AIRSPACE.

SCRAMBLE THE TALONS. WE WILL INTERCEPT.
WE ANTICIPATED YOUR ORDER, MY KING. BUT BEFORE WE COULD MAKE CONTACT... THE PLANE EXPLODED.
&#$%#$& CALLED IT!

SEE, T'CHALLA?! I TOLD YOU HOW THIS WAS ALL GONNA GO DOWN!

"AND NOW IT'S GOING DOWN!"
APPROACHING WAKANDAN AIRSPACE. MINUTES AGO.
IT WAS MAX BOGUS OF DEADPOOL TO CUT YOUR ARM OFF, BRO.

AND HE DIDN'T EVEN SIGN YOUR HAT.
IT'S ALL GOOD, BROHEIM. WHEN DAD SEES MY EPIC BATTLE-DAMAGE, HE'LL HAVE TO HUG ME.
HE MIGHT EVEN HUG BOTH OF US!
I DUNNO, DUDE. HE MIGHT BE PRETTY P.O.'D THAT YOU CALLED BACK THE COMPANY JET EARLY.

BUT ISN'T THAT THE BEAUTY OF PRIVATE PLANES?
DUDE?

ALWAYS AVAILABLE. SO LITTLE SECURITY.
SO MANY LITTLE PLACES TO HIDE.
"OOH! IS THAT FOR HALLOWEEN?"

UBUSUKU BOKUFA. A GIFT FROM THE CHILDREN FOR OUR FESTIVAL FOR THE DEAD.
NO.
SO... WAKANDAN HALLOWEEN.
AGREE TO DISAGREE.

OOH--SHARP AND SHINY! SO WHAT'S THE PLAN HERE, CHALLY? YOU GONNA SEAM ME UP BEFORE YOU TEAM ME UP?
WE ARE NOT "TEAMING UP." BUT YOU ARE A MAGNET FOR CATASTROPHE--

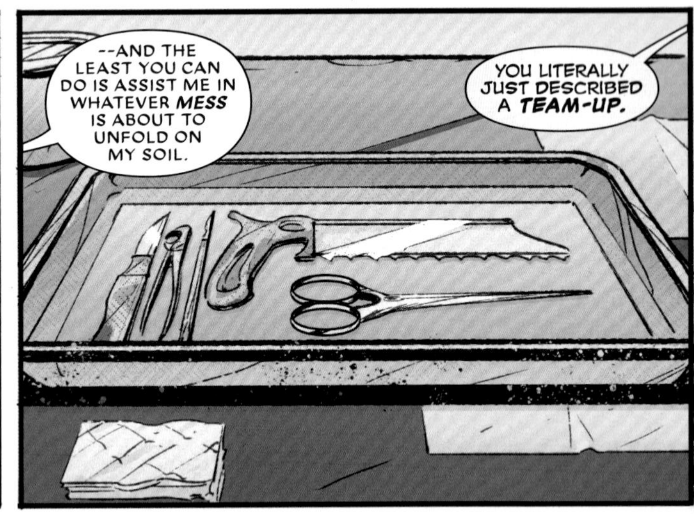
--AND THE LEAST YOU CAN DO IS ASSIST ME IN WHATEVER MESS IS ABOUT TO UNFOLD ON MY SOIL.
YOU LITERALLY JUST DESCRIBED A TEAM-UP.

IT'S LIKE I SAID, B.P., THERE'S A RHYTHM TO THESE SUPER HERO TEAM-UPS. FIRST, THE SMALL MISUNDERSTANDING. THEN, THE BIG FIGHT (WHICH WAS A TIE BY THE WAY).
SO YOU'D BETTER PATCH ME UP QUICK, BECAUSE WE BOTH KNOW WHAT HAPPENS IN ISSUE #3.

HEY, ARE YOU SURE IT'S NOT HALLOWEEN?

"BECAUSE **LITERALLY NO ONE** LOVES HALLOWEEN MORE THAN ME."

HEY, "JERK" O'LANTERN, HALLOWEEN WAS TWO MONTHS AGO!

BEFORE.
--SEVERE SPINAL TRAUMA! MOVE! MOVE! MOVE!
BURNS EVERYWHERE-- OLD BURNS, LIKE THEY WERE NEVER TREATED!
SOMEBODY TAKE THIS STUPID THING! I THINK IT'S HIS "HEAD."

THEN.
--SHOULDN'T BE ALIVE. AND AFTER READING YOUR FILE, I'D LIKE TO KILL YOU MYSELF. WASTE OF ALL THAT RECONSTRUCTIVE SURGERY IF YOU ASK ME.
BUT WE NEED TEST SUBJECTS FOR A NEW "REHABILITATION PROGRAM." THINK OF IT AS--

LATER.
--WITNESS PROTECTION. BUT FOR THE MIND.
OH, AND WE'LL NEED YOU TO TAKE THESE. ALL OF THEM.

SO.
EVERY DAY! THAT'S HOW OFTEN SOMETHING CRAZY HAPPENS HERE AT MANHATTAN DIRECT MAIL SALES AND SERVICES.
OH, AND CALL ME LARRY. EVERYONE DOES... WHEN THEY'RE NOT TOO BUSY LAUGHING! WELCOME ABOARD, UH--SORRY, WHAT WAS YOUR NAME AGAIN?

FINALLY.
EEP
OSED
JACK! THESE NEED TO GO OUT BEFORE FIVE!
JACK? ARE YOU EVEN LISTENING TO ME?

HONESTY.
INTEGRITY.
ORMANCE.
HUH? OH, SORRY.
MY HEAD WAS SOMEWHERE ELSE.
CLERICAL OPERATIONS AMBASSADOR LVL. 1
ATE
AYS
BLACK PANTHER VS. DEADPOOL
PART THREE: A MUTUAL THREAT!

A FEW DAYS AGO.
MY NAME IS JACK. I USED TO BE JACK O'LANTERN.
EXPENSE REPORTS... LARRY'S YOGURT...
UH-HUH. UH-HUH.
THEN I DIED.

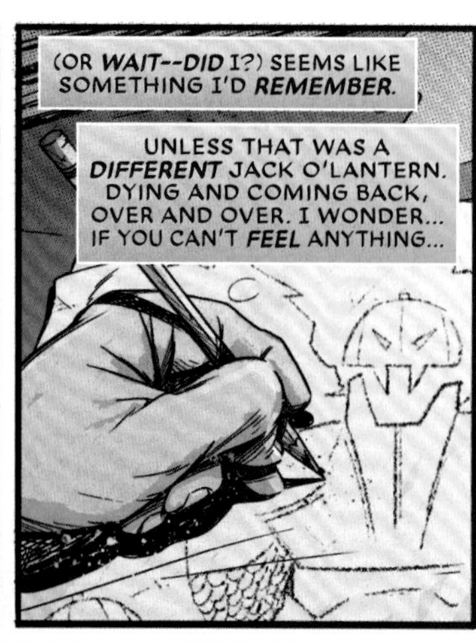
(OR WAIT--DID I?) SEEMS LIKE SOMETHING I'D REMEMBER.
UNLESS THAT WAS A DIFFERENT JACK O'LANTERN. DYING AND COMING BACK, OVER AND OVER. I WONDER... IF YOU CAN'T FEEL ANYTHING...

...HOW CAN YOU TELL WHEN YOU'RE ALIVE AND WHEN YOU'RE DEAD?
HEY. THAT'S DEADPOOL. I KNOW HIM.

(DO I KNOW HIM?)
THAT IS DEADPOOL DRESSED LIKE AN ELEPHANT. I WONDER WHERE HE'S GOING.
SOMEPLACE COOL, I BET.

DEADPOOL DOESN'T WONDER IF HE'S ALIVE OR DEAD.
DEADPOOL JUST LIVES.

WHERE ARE YOU GOING?
SCOOOOCH

I'M GONNA GO KILL LARRY.

HAW! KILL HIM A LITTLE EXTRA FOR ME, WILL YA?
OKAY.

AAAUUUGGH!!!
AAAAUUGGGGGGH!!!
"MAN. THIS IS MESSED UP."

WAKANDA. NOW.
AGREED. I WILL NEVER FORGIVE YOU FOR FORCING ME TO BRING THIS ABOMINATION INTO THE WORLD.
BLEH!
AWWW, SHURI! YOU SOUND JUST LIKE MY MOM.
"SO. AN AMERICAN PRIVATE JET HAS EXPLODED OVER WAKANDA, AND THIS VIBRANIUM-CRAZED ASSASSIN HAS INFILTRATED THE PALACE, TWICE."

YES, MOTHER, THAT'S ABOUT THE SIZE OF IT. *OKOYE* IS LOOKING INTO THE PLANE, WHILE I KEEP AN EYE ON THE *PRESENT* DANGER.
QUITE A DAY.
YOU HAD A QUESTION, BEFORE WE WERE SO COLORFULLY INTERRUPTED.

YOU WANT TO KNOW IF YOU ARE THE *GREATEST* OF THE BLACK PANTHERS?
OF COURSE YOU ARE. YOU ARE MY *SON*.

NOW TELL ME WHAT YOU *ACTUALLY* WISH TO TELL ME.

I COMBINED A *SELF-REGENERATING* CELL SAMPLE FROM OUR *GUEST* WITH THE SAME *ARTIFICIAL STEM CELLS* THAT SHURI IS USING TO HEAL THAT ZEBRA. THERE WAS A *REACTION*.
...I BELIEVE I HAVE *CURED DEATH.*

I SEE. WELL.
OUR FAMILY KNOWS BETTER THAN MOST...

"...DEATH IS NOT WHAT IT USED TO BE."
A FEW DAYS AGO (OR A FEW MINUTES AFTER LARRY).
BRONX ZOO
EXCUSE ME!

I WAS FOLLOWING A MAN, DRESSED AS A SUPER-ASSASSIN, DRESSED AS AN ELEPHANT. HE GOT ON YOUR TRUCK.

BRONX ZOO
I--I DON'T KNOW WHAT YOU'RE TALKING ABOUT, PAL, BUT ANY ELEPHANTS ON THAT TRUCK ARE ON THEIR WAY TO *WAKANDA*.
IS THAT COFFEE OR BLOOD?

WAKANDA.
DEADPOOL IS GOING TO WAKANDA. COOL.

BRONX ZOO
THANKS.
THAT'S WHAT *I'LL* DO. I'LL DIG OUT MY *THINGS* FROM THE BUS STATION LOCKER. I'LL SNEAK ONTO A PLANE. AND I'LL GO TO WAKANDA.
MAYBE DEADPOOL WILL *KILL* ME FOR REAL. HE LIKES DOING THAT.

OR MAYBE I'LL JUST KILL DEADPOOL.
DID YOU HEAR ME?
HM?

I SAID I'VE BEEN READING QUITE A LOT ABOUT FRANCE LATELY.
FRANCE? I THOUGHT YOU WERE STUDYING THE HISTORY OF ANCIENT CHINA?
I FINISHED CHINA.
YOU'RE AWARE OF LOUIS XIV?

I DO NOT HAVE TIME TO READ ABOUT DEAD WHITE KINGS.

THERE ARE LESSONS IN THE FAILURES OF THOSE WHO CAME BEFORE YOU.
LOUIS XIV CONSOLIDATED THE POWER OF THE MONARCHY, ANOINTING HIMSELF THE SUN KING, AROUND WHOM ALL OTHERS ORBITED.
HE BUILT VERSAILLES, FOSTERED ART AND LITERATURE, AND WAS BELOVED AS THESE THINGS GO.
HE REIGNED WITH ABSOLUTE POWER FOR 72 YEARS.

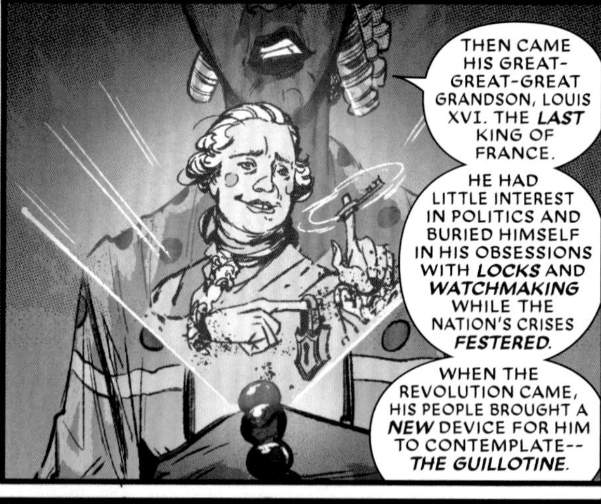
THEN CAME HIS GREAT-GREAT-GREAT GRANDSON, LOUIS XVI. THE LAST KING OF FRANCE.
HE HAD LITTLE INTEREST IN POLITICS AND BURIED HIMSELF IN HIS OBSESSIONS WITH LOCKS AND WATCHMAKING WHILE THE NATION'S CRISES FESTERED.
WHEN THE REVOLUTION CAME, HIS PEOPLE BROUGHT A NEW DEVICE FOR HIM TO CONTEMPLATE-- THE GUILLOTINE.

WHY DO YOU TELL ME THIS?
BECAUSE BOTH KINGS WERE MEN OF THEIR TIME.
PERHAPS, T'CHALLA, IF YOU TAKE THIS "CURE," YOU COULD BE A MAN FOR ALL TIME. IF ANYONE COULD DO IT, IT WOULD BE YOU.

PEOPLE MUST BE PROTECTED, T'CHALLA, BUT THEY MUST ALSO BE GIVEN THE FREEDOM TO *CHANGE*.

AND HISTORICALLY, A KING WHO DOES NOT CHANGE ALONGSIDE HIS PEOPLE...

!?

"PERHAPS ONE FOREIGN INVADER CAN HELP ME FIGHT ANOTHER."
HELLO!

*TRANSLATED FROM WAKANDAN.
‹WHAT ARE YOU? WHAT DO YOU WANT?›*
RELAX! "I COME IN PEACE." HEH.
ARE THOSE RHINOS? I'VE NEVER SEEN A RHINO BEFORE. (HAVE I?)

IT'S ALL FUZZY.
I'M NOT GOING TO KILL YOU, BY THE WAY. YOU'D PROBABLY JUST COME BACK, ANYHOW.
THAT'S WHAT HAPPENED TO ME. NOW I JUST WANT TO LIVE, LIKE DEADPOOL DOES. DO YOU UNDERSTAND? I WANT TO FEEL.

I WANT TO KILL SOMETHING THAT WON'T COME BACK.

WOO-HOO! WHO HAS TWO THUMBS (AGAIN) AND IS GOING ON A CLASSIC MARVEL TEAM-UP?!
I THOUGHT YOU SAID THIS WAS "A MUTUAL THREAT."
EH, IF I'M BEING HONEST WITH MYSELF, IT'S KIND OF THE SAME BEAT.
VOOOOM!!
SO WHAT'S THE PLAN? I HELP STOP THIS BAD GUY, AND YOU'RE SO GRATEFUL THAT YOU GIVE ME AN OUNCE OF VIBRANIUM FOR MY TROUBLE?
NO.
WHY CAN'T YOU JUST TRUST THAT I NEED IT FOR A GOOD REASON?
WILLIE LUMPKIN.
THE MAN YOU PUT ON LIFE SUPPORT. HOSPITAL RECORDS RECOMMEND VIBRANIUM THERAPY.
YOU KNEW THIS WHOLE TIME?!
IF THERE IS A CAMERA, WAKANDA IS WATCHING. AND LUMPKIN IS A FRIEND OF A FRIEND.
THEN WHY NOT JUST GIVE ME THE VIBRANIUM SO WE CAN GO SAVE HIM?

BECAUSE IT WON'T WORK.
BUT--BUT THE DOCTOR SAID IT CURED TONY STARK!
STARK IS AN IMPROBABLY HEALTHY BILLIONAIRE WHO COULDN'T KILL HIMSELF IF HE TRIED--AND HE'S TRIED.
LUMPKIN IS A SEPTUAGENARIAN MAILMAN IN A CITY HOSPITAL. THEY CANNOT REPLICATE THE TREATMENT.
IF LUMPKIN COULD BE SAVED, REED RICHARDS WOULD DO IT. AND HE'S NOT PLEASED WITH YOU, BY THE WAY.
BEEP. BEEP. BOOP.
IF YOU TRULY WISH TO REDEEM YOURSELF, YOU CAN START BY HELPING ME SAVE LIVES HERE AND NOW.
BUT LUMPKIN'S DEATH IS ONE YOU MUST LEARN TO LIVE WITH. HIS ODDS ARE A MILLION TO ONE. LESS.
A MILLION TO ONE? IS THAT ALL?! AND YOU SAY I'M NOT A BELIEVER.
I GUESS THAT'S THE DIFFERENCE BETWEEN US.
I BELIEVE--

--IN REALITY.
EXACTLY!!!

HEY, DOES ANYONE ELSE SMELL BARBECUE? I'D KILL FOR SOME BRISKET RIGHT NOW.
WHY AM I THE ONLY COMIC BOOK CHARACTER WHO EVER STOPS FOR LUNCH?
‹I SAW THE SMOKE. ARE YOU HURT?›

‹HE...HE SAID HE DIDN'T WANT US...›
OH MAN, T'CHALLA. YOU WANT THE GOOD NEWS FIRST? 'CUZ I FOUND THE BARBECUE.

FOOOSH!
BUT THIS SURE AS HECK AIN'T BRISKET.

WHAT KIND OF ANIMAL WOULD DO THIS?!
IT'S MESSED UP, RIGHT? LIKE, I AM DEFINITELY NOT PROUD OF HOW HUNGRY THIS IS MAKING ME.
HEY, B.P.-- ARE YOU POSITIVE IT'S NOT HALLOWEEN?

'CUZ I DON'T GET WHY A RHINO FARM WOULD NEED A SCARECROW.

THAT'S JACK O'LANTERN, YOU IDIOT!
HEY! DON'T YOU DARE CALL ME AN--

CHUNK
--ARGLEBLAT.

YOUR MAJESTY.
I SEE YOU GOT MY SMOKE SIGNAL.

MONSTER!
YESSSS!

MONSTER! GHOULIE!

THE THING THAT GOES THUMP IN THE NIGHT!

THE STUFF OF NIGHTMARES!

SHUCK
MARZIPAN!

DEADPOOL!
I FOLLOWED YOU HERE, YOU KNOW.
YOU WHAT?!

I USED TO LOOK LIKE YOU-- (DID I?)--BURNED AND BROKEN. DEAD AND WALKING.
UNALIVE.

DON'T YOU SEE? HELL WON'T HAVE US! THERE'S NO ROOM LEFT IN THE CEMETERY!
PITY.
FWOOSH

WE'LL HAVE TO CREMATE.
FWOOSH

GOOD KITTY! NOW YOU! BLOG POSTER!
BLACK PANTHER.
YES! HELP BRAIN BOO-BOO!
KOFF KOFF
THUMP!

PLUCK
UFF!

UGH. THANKS. I HATE LOBOTOMIES.
THAT THING SAID IT FOLLOWED YOU HERE.
I'M ALIVE. I KNOW IT NOW.

OH YEAH, MISTER HIGH-AND-MIGHTY, WE'RE CLEARLY BEST PALS.
SETTING ME ON FIRE AND STABBING ME IN THE BRAIN IS OUR SECRET HANDSHAKE.
JUST MAKE SURE HE'S SUBDUED. I'LL CHECK ON THE FAMILY.
EVERYTHING HURTS.

AFTER THAT, WE WILL HAVE WORDS.
EVERYTHING BURNS.
SHEATH

I DID IT, THOUGH, DIDN'T I? DEADPOOL AND THE BLACK PANTHER. THIS WILL BE A STORY.
THIS EVIL MAN IS DEALT WITH. WE WILL DO OUR BEST TO RESTORE WHAT HE TOOK.
A MONSTER STORY.

I PROMISE YOU, WE WILL TAKE HIM BACK TO THE CITY AND LOCK HIM IN THE DEEPEST--
WHAT? WHAT'S WRONG?
AND STORIES NEVER--

NO!
BLAM

WHAT DID YOU DO?!
WHAT? YOU TOLD ME TO *STOP* THE *BAD GUY!*

PUNFCH

THIS IS HOW YOU REPAY MY TRUST?!
OKAY, I AM GETTING SOME REAL *MIXED MESSAGES* HERE.

ERK! YOU REALLY LOVE GOING FOR THE JUGULAR, DON'T YOU?
I SAID SUBDUE HIM! SO THAT HE COULD FACE JUSTICE!
THAT IS WHAT A HERO WOULD DO.

I DID NOT TELL YOU TO COMMIT MURDER IN FRONT OF A CHILD!
ARE YOU SERIOUS? YOU REALLY WANTED TO FLY BACK WITH A MURDEROUS LUNATIC ON BOARD?
...
YOUNG MAN, PLEASE RETURN TO YOUR MOTHER AND GO INSIDE.
YOU HAVE SEEN ENOUGH TODAY.

WE COULD'VE SKIPPED ALL THIS, IF YOU'D JUST TRUSTED-- OOF!
IT'S MY FAULT FOR TURNING MY BACK ON YOU.
WHAM!

MY MOTHER WAS WRONG.
HEY! THOSE ARE PERSONAL ITEMS!
AS LONG AS THERE IS EVIL IN THIS WORLD THAT CANNOT DIE, THERE MUST BE SOMEONE HERE TO STOP IT.
SHOONF

THERE WAS NEVER A "MUTUAL THREAT." YOU ARE THE THREAT!
I'M WARNING YOU, WHISKERS. TAKE ONE MORE STEP...
AND WHAT? YOU'LL KILL ME?
THAT'S THE DIFFERENCE BETWEEN US, WADE WILSON.

I KNOW THIS WON'T KILL YOU.
CLIFFHANGER!

HEY, T'CHALLA--
--HOW YOU LIKE MEOW?

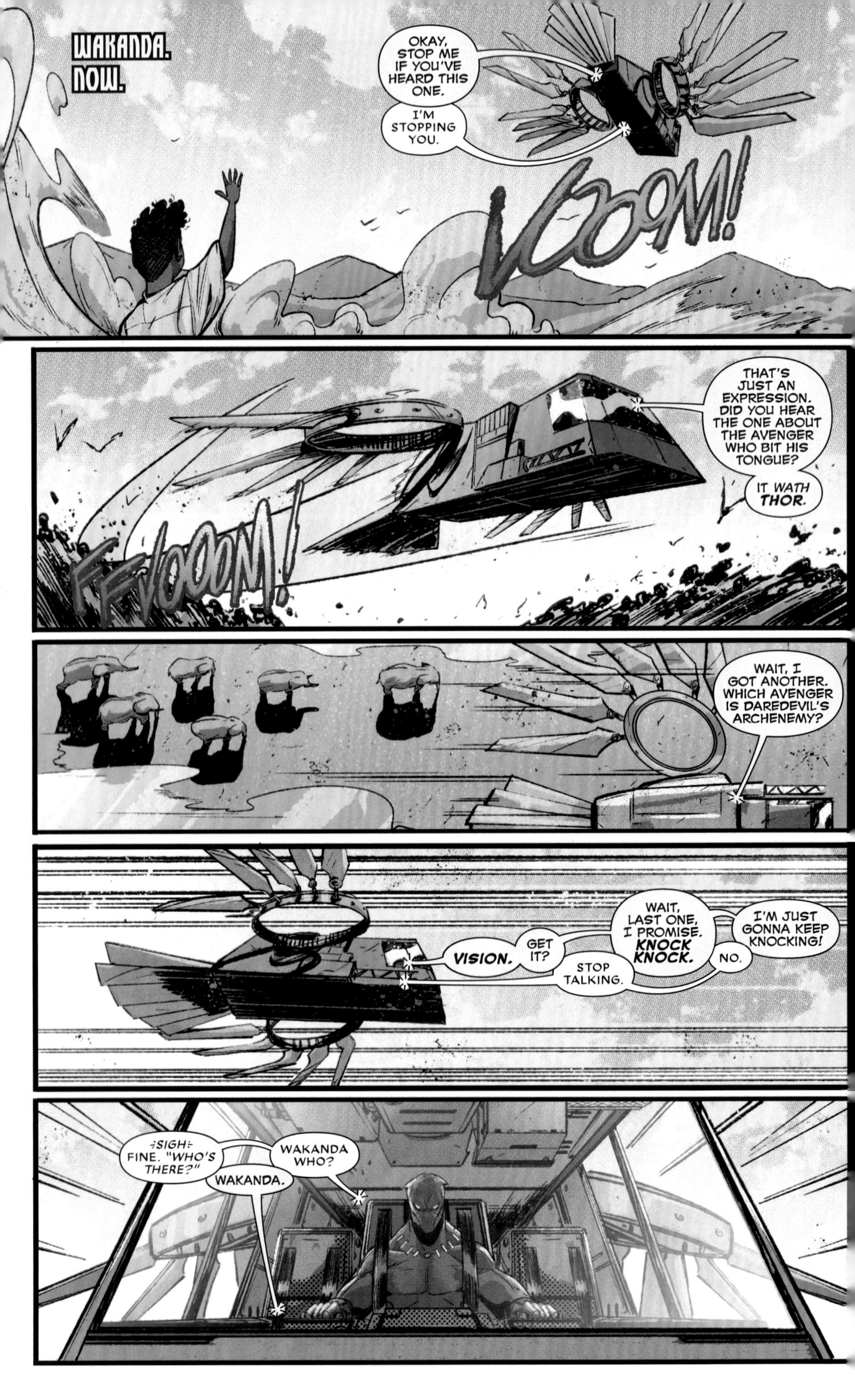
WAKANDA. NOW.
OKAY, STOP ME IF YOU'VE HEARD THIS ONE.
I'M STOPPING YOU.
VOOOM!
THAT'S JUST AN EXPRESSION. DID YOU HEAR THE ONE ABOUT THE AVENGER WHO BIT HIS TONGUE?
IT WATH THOR.
FFVOOOM!
WAIT, I GOT ANOTHER. WHICH AVENGER IS DAREDEVIL'S ARCHENEMY?
VISION.
GET IT?
STOP TALKING.
WAIT, LAST ONE, I PROMISE. KNOCK KNOCK.
NO.
I'M JUST GONNA KEEP KNOCKING!
SIGH FINE. "WHO'S THERE?"
WAKANDA.
WAKANDA WHO?

"WAKANDA" PERSON CUTS OFF A DUDE'S HEAD?!
BLACK PANTHER VS. DEADPOOL
PART FOUR: A CLASSIC MARVEL TEAM-UP! OR SOMETHING

YOU SAID IT YOURSELF. IT WAS UNSAFE TO FLY BACK TO WAKANDA WITH A HOMICIDAL MANIAC ON BOARD.
I MEANT JACK O'LANTERN! AND YOU SHOULD BE THANKING ME FOR PUNCHING THAT DUDE'S CARD. I ALREADY GOT PAST YOUR SECURITY TWICE AND I'M ONE OF THE GOOD GUYS.

SO YOU KEEP TELLING YOURSELF.
HEY, CAN I ASK YOU A QUESTION?
NO.
IT'S GOING TO BE A LONG TRIP IF WE CAN'T CHIT-CHAT.
IT ALREADY IS.

I MEANT FOR ME.
ISN'T "BLACK PANTHER" KIND OF REDUNDANT? I MEAN, AREN'T ALL PANTHERS BLACK?
HOP!
HOP!

MY HONORIFICS DO NOT TRANSLATE CLEANLY INTO SIMPLER LANGUAGES. TO THE OUTSIDE WORLD, I AM "THE BLACK PANTHER."
TO MY PEOPLE, I AM DAMISA-SARKI-- SIMPLY "THE PANTHER."

OH, RIGHT. I GUESS TA-NEHISI COATES KIND OF ADDRESSED IT.
YES, WE SPEAK FREQUENTLY.
WAIT! YOU GOT THAT REFERENCE?! I THOUGHT I WAS THROWING THAT ONE AT THE FOURTH WALL FOR SURE!

AGAIN, YOU'VE LOST ME. BUT MR. COATES' WORK HAS TAUGHT ME MUCH ABOUT THE AMERICAN PSYCHE.

SO FORGIVE ME IF I DON'T ENTIRELY TRUST YOU.
WHY DOES EVERYONE FORGET THAT I'M CANADIAN?

PROBABLY BECAUSE I'VE NEVER HAD ANYTHING TO SAY "SO-RRY" ABOUT.
GUARDS, PLEASE COLLECT THE REST OF HIM.

PLOP!
WOO-HOO! AVENGER ASSEMBLED!

YOU'RE NOT AN AVENGER.
ARE YOU KIDDING? I'M AN EVERYTHING! AVENGER. X-MAN. THINKING ABOUT BECOMING A DEFENDER, TBH.
HEY, THANKS FOR PUTTING ME BACK TOGETHER. YOU DIDN'T HAVE TO DO THAT.

I KNOW. I COULDN'T RISK YOU ESCAPING IN A NEW BODY.
OR GROWING A SECOND MOUTH.
WHAT ARE ALL THESE POUCHES FOR?

DON'T KNOCK THE POUCHES, MAN. I GOT EVERYTHING IN THOSE BABIES. SERIOUSLY, READ ISSUE #1 ALREADY.
SO, YOU'VE GOT ME STRAPPED DOWN IN YOUR OBVIOUS SEX DUNGEON. WHAT HAPPENS NEXT?
I CALL THE INTERNATIONAL AUTHORITIES, AND YOU STAND TRIAL FOR MURDER.

ORRRRR... I GIVE YOU ONE LAST CHANCE TO GIVE ME THE VIBRANIUM I NEED TO SAVE WILLIE LUMPKIN'S LIFE.
AND YOU LET ME GO!

YOU'RE JOKING.
USUALLY! BUT NO.
I TOLD YOU, THE VIBRANIUM THERAPY, IT'S--
"A MILLION-TO-ONE ODDS." I KNOW.

KINDA LIKE DEADPOOL PULLING A FAST ONE ON THE BLACK PANTHER.

WHAT ARE YOU TALKING ABOUT?
YOU KNOW, YOU'VE SAID SOME HURTFUL THINGS DURING OUR LITTLE PLAYDATE.
BUT YOU'RE RIGHT. I DON'T HAVE A COUNTRY. OR A FAMILY. OR "THE WEIGHT OF MY OWN DEATH" OR WHATEVER.

BUT WHAT I DO HAVE IS A POUCH FULL OF C-4 ON A 24-HOUR DEAD MAN'S SWITCH.
AND IF I DON'T HIT THE BUTTON IN A FEW SECONDS... KABOOM.

WHICH ONE, DAMMIT?! WHY DO YOU HAVE SO MANY POUCHES!!!
SORRY FOR T'CHEATING, T'CHALLA, BUT I'M ON A DEADLINE HERE.
WHAT'S THAT OLD SAYING ABOUT PLAYING WITH SOMEONE WHO HAS NOTHING TO LOSE?

OH, RIGHT. "DON'T."

KABOOM!
THUMPF!

BRILLIANT MOVE, DP! DEFINITELY NOT A TOTAL FLUKE. BUT WE STILL NEED AN ESCAPE PLAN.
STEP ONE: DISLOCATE EVERYTHING AND HOUDINI MY WAY OUTTA THIS "FIFTY SHADES" SITUATION.

STEP TWO: GRAB WHATEVER GEAR ISN'T 'SPLODED.
!!
BETTER BRING THE WRECKER'S MAGIC CROWBAR IN CASE I GOTTA DO A LITTLE BREAKING AND EXITING.

STEPS THREE-THROUGH-QUESTION MARK: STEAL THE MOST PRECIOUS SUBSTANCE ON EARTH FROM THE SMARTEST MAN ON EARTH AND ESCAPE FROM THE MOST ADVANCED COUNTRY ON EARTH.

LIKE I SAID.
PIECE OF CAKE.

NO.

THIS TIME THE VILLAIN FACES JUSTICE.
DAMISA-SARKI TRACKS THE *SOUL*, NOT THE BODY.
BUT DEADPOOL HAS SHED *MANY* BODIES.

NOW WE FIND OUT IF HE STILL HAS A *SOUL*.
HEY, YOU KNOW WHAT REALLY HONKS MY GRAPES?

WHO THE HELL WAS BLACK PANTHER TALKING TO JUST NOW?
HIMSELF? ME? YOU?

SURE, WHEN I DO IT, I'M "BREAKING THE FOURTH WALL." BUT WHEN LITERALLY EVERYONE ELSE DOES IT, IT'S CALLED "NARRATING."
TOTAL DOUBLE STANDARD.
SPEAKING OF BREAKING WALLS, I COULD SURE USE AN ESCAPE ROUTE ABOUT NOW.

DANG IT--TELEPORTER STILL ALL FZZT'D UP.
FZZT
FZZT
GONNA HAVE TO--

PRUNCH

DAMMIFF, MY NOFE!
STOP PUNFFING ME!
YOU CANNOT ESCAPE ME. I AM WAKANDA.
SUBMIT.
SPOOT
FINE. I'M NOT AN IDIOT, OKAY?
I KNOW I CAN'T ACTUALLY BEAT THE BLACK &#$%&$# PANTHER.
BUT AT LEAST I CAN GO DOWN--
?!
FZZZT
--SWINGING?!
OH SWEET!
FZZT'ING TELEPORTER--
FZZT
--TO THE RESCUE!
EXPL--
NO!

--OITABLE GLITCH!
...?
HOLY PANTHER CAVE!

MUST BE T'CHALLA'S SECRET STASH OF HIGH-TECH CAT TOYS! OOH, SCIENCE BEADS.
THESE BABIES MUST BE MADE OF VIBRANIUM. "DON'T BOTHER WRAPPING IT UP FOR ME, MADAM."

"I'LL WEAR IT OUT!"
WAIT, WHY DO I FEEL TINGLY AGAIN?
AND WHY IS IT NEVER WHERE I WANT TO BE TINGLED?
DODOM!
FLASH!

OH GREAT, THE INSTRUCTIONS ARE IN WAKANDAN. THAT'S HELPFUL.
ENGLISH DETECTED. PROTOTYPE PANTHER SUIT INITIALIZING.
*WAKANDAN FOR "CALIBRATING."

INSTALLING KIMOYO TECH UPGRADE.
"KIMOYO TECH"? SO THIS THING HAS WI-FI? AND ITS OWN WAKANDAN SIRI?
OR WOULD THAT BE SHURI?
COMMAND NOT RECOGNIZED. SCANNING DNA.

YIKES, BUY A GUY A DRINK FIRST.
DNA IDENTIFIED: WADE WILSON. DEADPOOL.
CUSTOMIZING SETTINGS.

HUH? WAKANDAN AGAIN?
NO OFFENSE, "SHIRI," BUT HOW DO I PRESS 2 FOR ENGLISH?
*"SUIT CALIBRATED."

WELCOME, DEADPOOL.
NO. NOT DEADPOOL. MEET... PANTHERPOOL.
OR DEAD PANTHER? NO, PANTHERPOOL. PANTHERPOOL'S BETTER.
FLASSH

I SAID SUBMIT!
VERRSH!

EEP! NOT IN MY NEW FACE!
VERRSH!

HEY! YOUR DEADPOOL-DISMEMBERMENT GIZMO CAN'T SLICE THROUGH THIS SUIT!
THANKS FOR THE MATCHING THREADS, BP! YOU THINKING WHAT I'M THINKING?
FAKOOOM!

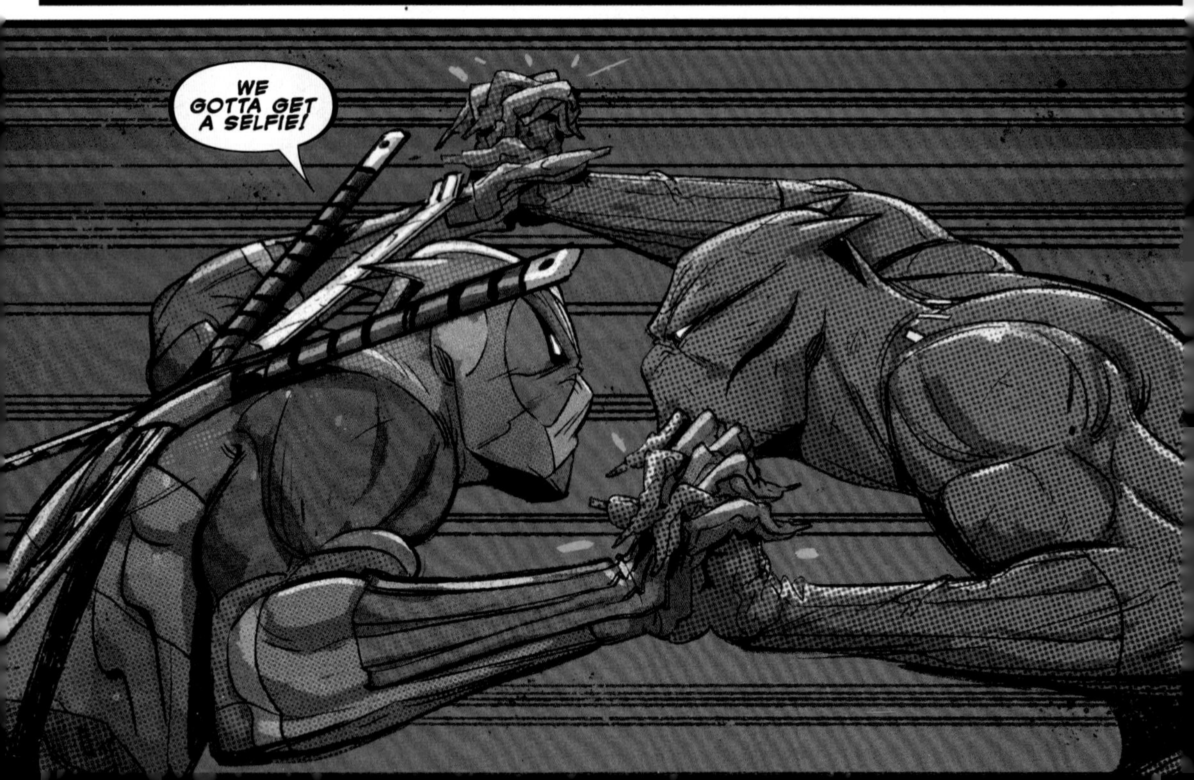
WE GOTTA GET A SELFIE!

RETURN THIS PROTOTYPE AND I MIGHT RECONSIDER SHOOTING YOUR HEAD INTO THE SUN!
ARE YOU KIDDING? GIVE UP NOW THAT WE'RE FINALLY EVENLY MATCHED? IN FACT...

...I MIGHT HAVE THE UPPER HAND!

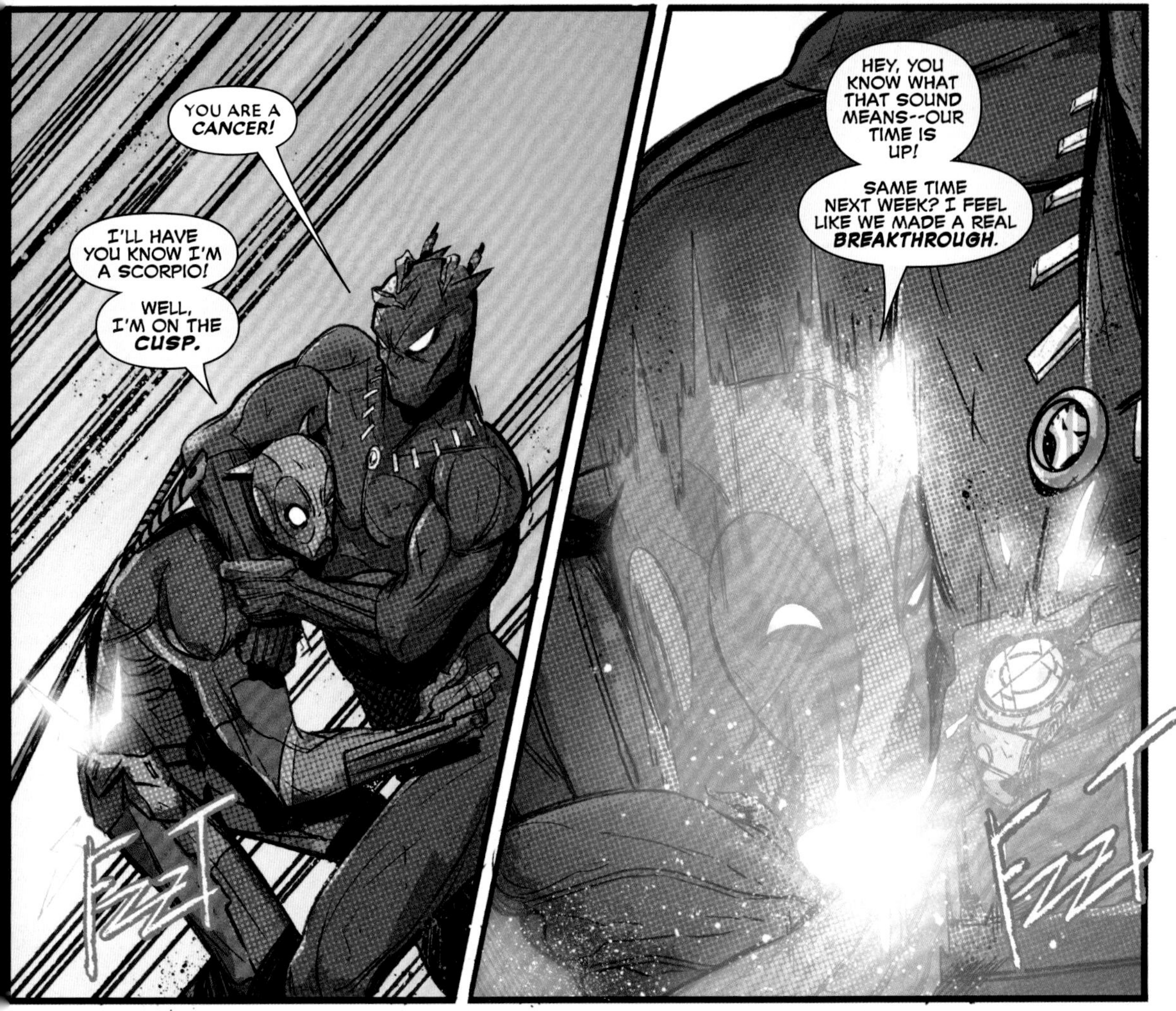
YOU ARE A CANCER!
I'LL HAVE YOU KNOW I'M A SCORPIO!
WELL, I'M ON THE CUSP.
FZZT
HEY, YOU KNOW WHAT THAT SOUND MEANS--OUR TIME IS UP!
SAME TIME NEXT WEEK? I FEEL LIKE WE MADE A REAL BREAKTHROUGH.
FZZT

NOT AGAIN!
PANTHER SUIT, ACTIVATE FLIGHT MODE! FLIGHT MODE!
COMMAND NOT RECOGNIZED.

SPLOOSH
$#%&!

UGH. I'VE BEEN A CAT FOR ABOUT FIVE MINUTES AND I ALREADY HATE WATER.
SHIRI, WHERE ARE WE?
SCANNING.

MENA NGAI-- "THE GREAT MOUND." SPIRITUAL AND ECONOMIC EPICENTER OF WAKANDA. WORLD'S LARGEST VIBRANIUM MINE.
FACE IT, PANTHER...I JUST HIT THE JACKPOT.

WELL, I'M A MAN OF MY WORD. I ONLY NEED ABOUT AN INCH TO SAVE WILLIE LUMPKIN. OF COURSE, TIPPING IS CUSTOMARY.

ONE THING I NEVER UNDERSTOOD, THOUGH--HOW DO YOU MINE A METAL THAT ABSORBS IMPACT?
HMM. IF ANYTHING CAN BREAK OFF A PIECE, IT'S THE WRECKER'S MAGIC CROWBAR.

I GUESS IT DID END UP BEING SIGNIFICANT TO THE PLOT!

KATAAAANG

JEEPERS! IT'S LIKE THE WHOLE MOUNTAIN IS REACTING TO THE CROWBAR'S ENCHANTED METAL AND RESONATING AT SOME MYSTERIOUS FREQUENCY!
AND NOW MY UNPREDICTABLE BROKEN TELEPORTER IS UNLEASHING A HUGE AMOUNT OF TELEPORTATION ENERGY!
RUMM RUMM RUMM RUMM RUMM RUMM RUMM

RUMM RUMM RUMM RUMM
RUMM RUMM RUMM RUMM
WHAT ARE THE ODDS?!

A MILLION TO ONE.
THE ODDS THAT DEADPOOL COULD BEST ME ON MY OWN TERRITORY, EVEN TEMPORARILY.
NO MATTER. HE *WILL* FACE JUSTICE.

EVEN IF IT TAKES 1,000 YEARS. IN FACT, I MAY *INSIST* THAT IT DOES.
YOUR MAJESTY.

OKOYE. HAVE WE FOUND HIM?
WE TRACKED THE *SUIT* TO THE GREAT MOUND. HE TELEPORTED INTO THE MINES, DEEP INSIDE THE MOUNTAIN.

INSULT UPON INSULT.
MOBILIZE THE *HATUT ZERAZE*. I WILL NOT MAKE THE MISTAKE OF ACTING *ALONE* AGAIN. I WANT THE MOUNTAIN *SURROUNDED*.
MY KING, THAT'S JUST IT. WE TRACKED HIM AS *FAR* AS THE MOUNTAIN.

BUT THE MOUNTAIN ITSELF... THE *ENTIRE* MOUNTAIN...

"IT'S GONE."
KA-
BRUNSTAD BURGERS
Paramus
N. Jersey
32 miles
LEFT 2 LANES
New York
City
EXIT ONLY
-CHING!

AND I THOUGHT MY FAMILY REUNIONS WERE BRUTAL...

WAKANDA. FORMER SITE OF THE GREAT VIBRANIUM MOUND.
‹IT'S ALL GONE.›*
*TRANSLATED FROM WAKANDAN.

THE WORKERS ARE ACCOUNTED FOR AND INJURIES ARE MINOR, THANK BAST. BUT THE MOUNTAIN--
I SEE.
‹PLEASE TELL ME WHAT HAPPENED HERE.›

‹YOUR MAJESTY? I... IT HAPPENED SO QUICKLY. THE WHOLE MOUNTAIN BEGAN TO VIBRATE, LIKE BEING INSIDE OF A BELL.›
‹THEN THE GROUND BENEATH OUR FEET... VANISHED.›

WE'VE TRACED THE TELEPORTATION SIGNATURE. HOWEVER, I'M AFRAID EXTRACTION WILL BE COMPLICATED...
AGREED, OKOYE. A DIRECT INVASION OF THE UNITED STATES IS INADVISABLE AT THIS TIME. VERY WELL.
NEW
JERSEY

THEN I SHALL USE A SCALPEL...
SHING

"...AND WE'LL CUT OUT THIS CANCER ONCE AND FOR ALL."
BLACK PANTHER VS. DEADPOOL
CONCLUSION: TAKE DOWN THE BAD GUY!
VIBRANIUM FOR SALE!
VIBRANIUM FOR SALE!!
$1 MILLION PER POUND (OR BEST OFFER)
?
KBBL
JUST OUTSIDE PARAMUS, NEW JERSEY.

~~DEADPOOL.~~
PANTHER-POOL.
CURRENTLY WEARING A STOLEN PANTHER SUIT.
PIPING-HOT VIBRANIUM! FRESH OFF THE WORLD-FAMOUS WAKANDAN VIBRANIUM MOUND, NOW CONVENIENTLY RELOCATED TO NEW JERSEY, USA!
YOU, SIR! YOU LOOK LIKE A SMART YOUNG MAN!

ARE YOU THE REAL BLACK PANTHER?
OF COURSE! CAN YOU IMAGINE HOW INAPPROPRIATE THIS COSTUME WOULD BE IF I WEREN'T?
MIGHT I INTEREST YOU IN A FREE SAMPLE OF THE MOST VALUABLE SUBSTANCE IN THE UNIVERSE?
FOR REAL?

SURE! THAT IS, IF YOU'VE GOT ANY VIBRANIUM MINING TOOLS IN YOUR TRUNK? TURNS OUT CARVING OFF A HUNK OF A MATTER THAT ABSORBS IMPACT IS A REAL CATCH-22.
AND (AS YOU'VE PROBABLY GUESSED) I NEED A PIECE QUICK, FOR A MILLION-TO-ONE EXPERIMENTAL PROCEDURE TO SAVE THE LIFE OF A MORTALLY WOUNDED MAILMAN.

AW $#@&. NEVER MIND.

THE EXPERT HAS ARRIVED.

!?
THUD
WAIT-- ARE YOU THE REAL BLACK PANTHER?
LEAVE.

"CAN I HELP YOU, SIR?"
FOR SALE!!
$1 MILLION PER POUND (OR BEST OFFER)

LOOK, B.P.
I GET IT, OKAY?

YOU THINK I STOLE SOMETHING FROM YOU. SOMETHING PRICELESS TO YOUR PEOPLE.
RUMBLE RUMBLE RUMBLE

BUT I SWEAR...
...I HAD NO IDEA BOTH OUR MOVIE FRANCHISES WERE GOING TO USE THE SAME ARMS-CROSSED SUPER HERO SALUTE.
RUMBLE RUMBLE RUMBLE

AND YOU GOTTA ADMIT, IT LOOKS WAY MORE LIKE AN "X" THAN A PANTH--
DEADPOOL. BY MY POWER AS KING AND PROTECTOR OF WAKANDA, I DECLARE WAR.
WHAT A COINCIDENCE!

HONK HONK
I DECLARE TRUCK!
WAIT!

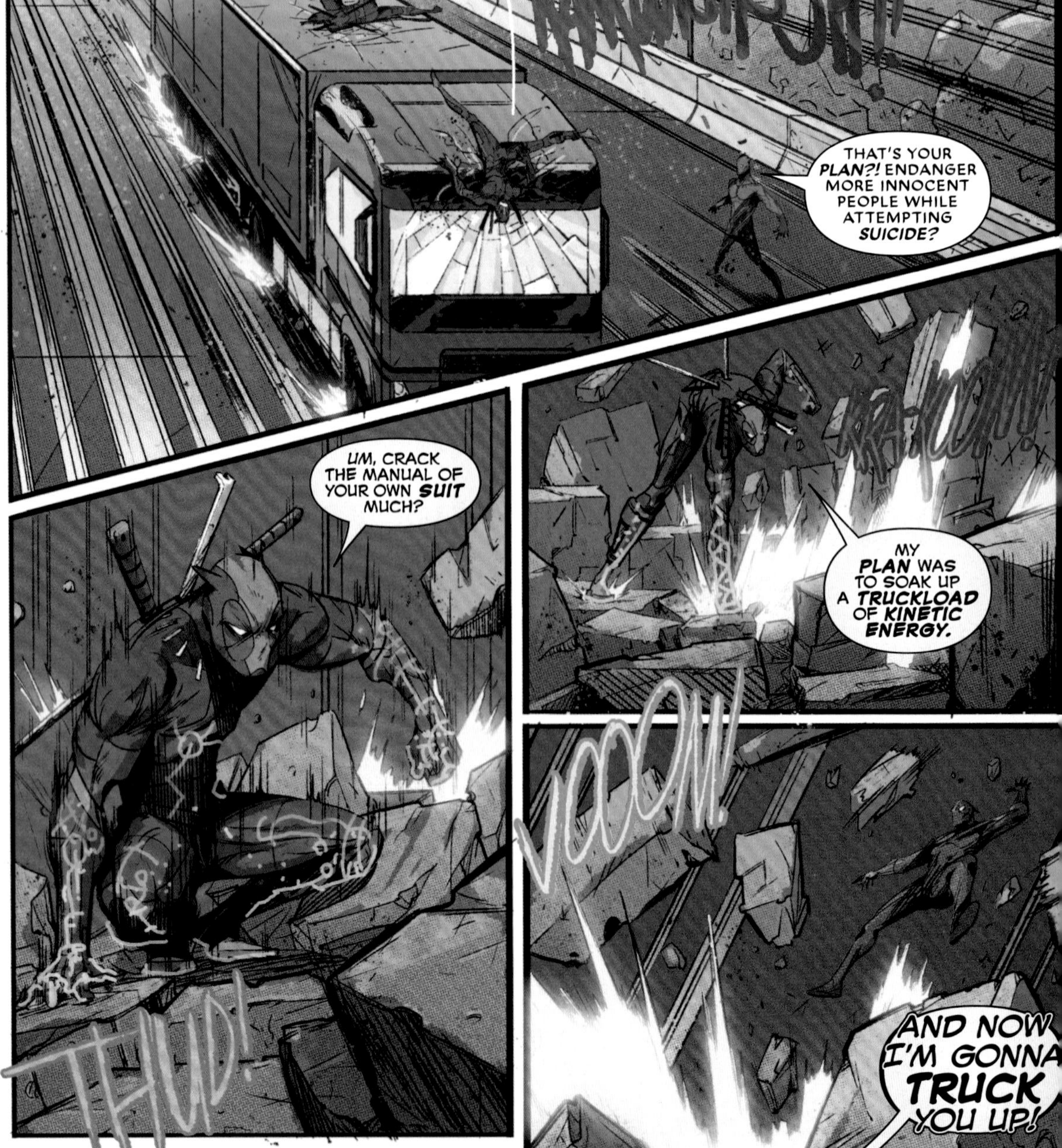
KAKRUNCHSH!!
THAT'S YOUR PLAN?! ENDANGER MORE INNOCENT PEOPLE WHILE ATTEMPTING SUICIDE?
UM, CRACK THE MANUAL OF YOUR OWN SUIT MUCH?
THUD!
MY PLAN WAS TO SOAK UP A TRUCKLOAD OF KINETIC ENERGY.
VOOOM!
AND NOW I'M GONNA TRUCK YOU UP!

OOF.
SHURI, PLEASE TELL ME YOU'RE PAYING ATTENTION.
WHAT DID I TELL YOU ABOUT WORRYING?

SHURI.
PRINCESS OF WAKANDA. SISTER OF THE BLACK PANTHER. DOES MACHINES.
I'M READING TOTAL ENERGY DEPLETION. HIS FIRE WALL IS DOWN. DEADPOOL HAS NO IDEA HOW TO USE THAT THING.
MY RIB CAGE DISAGREES.
STOP WHINING. YOU'RE LUCKY HE STOLE THE ONLY SUIT PROTOTYPE THAT CONNECTS TO THE INTERNET.

AND THE INTERNET IS WHERE I AM QUEEN.

SUIT OVERRIDE. PAIRING NEW USER.
NO! MY LICENSING OPPORTUNITIES!
SCHWOOP

BUT TO RETURN THE MOUNTAIN TO WAKANDA, I'LL NEED HIS TELEPORTER, AND THE WRECKER'S--
GRAB!
I KNOW.

DEADPOOL. THIS IS OVER.
GIVE ME THE CROWBAR.

'KAY.
KRANG!!
OKAY, CHEAP SHOT, BUT YOU ***TOTALLY*** SET ME UP FOR IT!
WUH-OH.

DEADPOOL! GET OUT OF THE ***ROAD!***
YOU'RE NOT THE KING OF ***ME!***
FWIP

CHURNK!
#&$%!

WEE-OOO-WEE-OOO
WEE-OOO-WEE-OOO
HONK! HONK! HONK!
HUFF WHAT IS IT WITH YOU AND JUMPING ON CARS?
WADE! YOU'RE PUTTING ALL THESE PEOPLE IN DANGER!
JUST GIVE ME THE CROWBAR AND THE TELEPORTER SO WE CAN END THIS!
NO! YOU GIVE ME A PIECE OF VIBRANIUM SO I CAN FIX EVERYTHING!

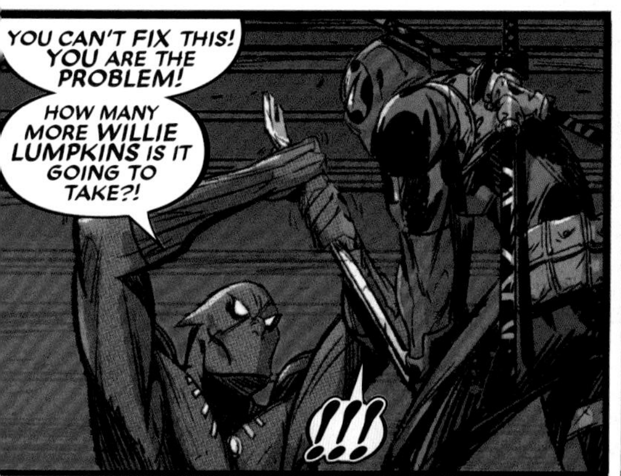
YOU CAN'T FIX THIS! YOU ARE THE PROBLEM!
HOW MANY MORE WILLIE LUMPKINS IS IT GOING TO TAKE?!
!!!

THAT'S IT, T'CHALLA. THIS ISN'T GONNA BE ONE OF THOSE B.S. SUPER HERO FIGHTS WHERE IT'S A "TIE"!
YOU'RE ON MY TERRITORY NOW! AND THIS TIME...

DEADPOOL WINS!!!

KRUNPHWCH!!
THIS WAS A MISTAKE.
I KNOW! CAN YOU IMAGINE SPENDING ETERNITY IN JERSEY?
SO-RRY, MRS. EPSTEIN.
I MEAN YOU SHOULD NOT HAVE BROUGHT ME HERE.
YOU HAVE DESECRATED A SACRED PLACE.
AND I AM MORE THAN THE KING OF WAKANDA.
I AM THE KING OF THE DEAD.
AND WHEREVER THE VEIL BETWEEN LIFE AND DEATH IS AT ITS THINNEST...

JACK
...IT IS ALWAYS MY TERRITORY.

WELCOME, DEADPOOL, TO THE LAND OF THE DEAD.
SEE NOW WHO YOU ARE TRULY UP AGAINST.
WHOA... ALL THE STARS...

WHA-WHAT DID YOU DO? THIS IS CHEATING! YOU'RE A CHEATER!
SHING
I CALLED UPON MY ANCESTORS, THE BLACK PANTHERS OF OLD.
AND NOW I UNDERSTAND WHY YOU STOPPED USING THAT TELEPORTER.

BECAUSE IT MADE THINGS TOO EASY! SEE DEADPOOL VOL. 2 #49!
ALSO BECAUSE THE WORD "BODYSLIDE" GAVE ME IDEAS ABOUT PLASTIC TARPS AND BABY OIL.
NO...

...YOU STOPPED BECAUSE YOU WERE AFRAID.

IT'S ONE THING TO GROW BACK A LIMB. A HEAD. EVEN COMING BACK FROM A DROP OF BLOOD.
BUT TO BE REASSEMBLED ELSEWHERE FROM ENTIRELY NEW MATTER?

HOW CAN YOU BE SURE THAT YOU'RE REALLY YOU?

PERHAPS YOU DIED--REALLY DIED--THE FIRST TIME YOU TELEPORTED. AND WHAT DOES THAT MAKE YOU NOW? A COPY OF A COPY.
SHUT UP! THE ONLY THING I'M A COPY OF IS DEATHSTRO--
DO NOT FEAR, WILSON. YOU STILL HAVE A SOUL.

IT'S BEEN WAITING FOR YOU HERE THE WHOLE TIME.
HEY, HANDSOME.
WHY THE WRONG FACE?!
?!!!

GOTTA BE HONEST, I'M A LITTLE MIFFED AT YOU.
YOU'RE OUT THERE IN THE LAND OF THE LIVING, PRETENDING TO STILL BE ME.
KLANG!

WHEN YOU'RE REALLY JUST A SOULLESS KILLING MACHINE.
I--I HAVE A SOUL! I'M A REAL BOY!

COME ON, MAN. HE'S THE BLACK #$%@#%& PANTHER. WE BOTH KNOW HOW THIS ENDS.
JUST GIVE HIM WHAT HE WANTS! AREN'T YOU TIRED? I KNOW I'M TIRED.

HOW MANY PEOPLE DO WE HAVE TO KILL BEFORE WE'RE FINALLY DONE?

...
OH MY GOD. IT'S TRUE. I MUST HAVE KNOWN ALL THIS TIME, BUT I NEVER REALLY BELIEVED IT UNTIL NOW.

I DO TALK TOO MUCH!!!

FLUMP!

CLANG!

END SIMULATION.

THE HOLOGRAM THINGY AGAIN. CLEVER.
TOTALLY KNEW THE WHOLE TIME.
HEY, T'CHALLA?

AM I A GOOD PERSON?

NO.
YEAH. I DIDN'T THINK SO. WELL, CONGRATS. YOU "TOOK DOWN THE BAD GUY."
"BLACK PANTHER WINS."

EVERY TIME I GET BLOWN TO PIECES, I THINK, "OKAY, WADE, YOU'RE A NEW MAN--LITERALLY! DON'T #$%@ IT UP THIS TIME!"
AND THEN I #$%@ IT UP.

IT'S JUST SO HARD TO ACTUALLY CHANGE.

AFTER ALL THE THINGS I'VE DONE...
THEY SAY YOU REALLY CAN SEE PEOPLE'S SOULS, T'CHALLA, AND...I GUESS I JUST WANNA KNOW...

CAN YOU STILL SEE MINE?
'CUZ I'M WORRIED IT'S THE ONE PART OF ME THAT DOESN'T GROW BACK.

...
I SEE A MAN WITH AN OPPORTUNITY TO MAKE THINGS RIGHT. YOU HAVE DONE MANY, MANY THINGS YOU CANNOT UNDO. BUT IF YOU TRULY WISH TO CHANGE?

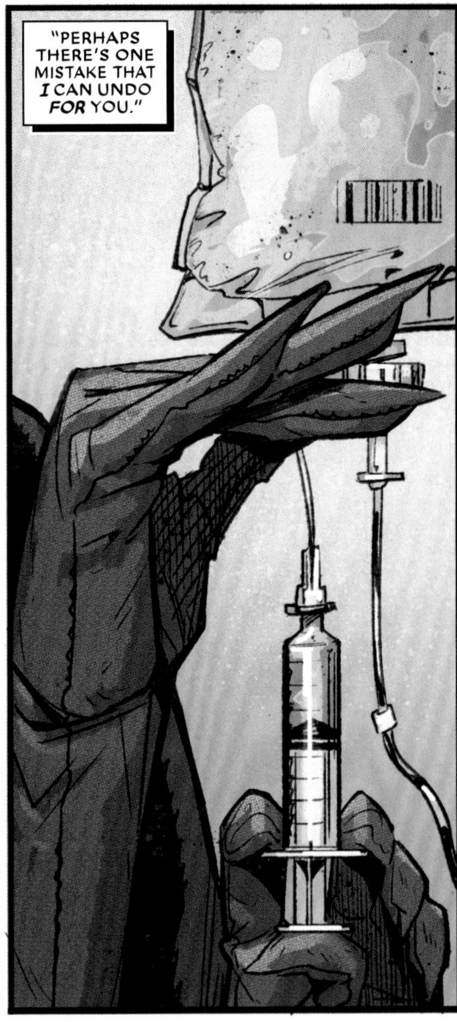
"PERHAPS THERE'S ONE MISTAKE THAT I CAN UNDO FOR YOU."

NOT MY FAULT
DR. RICHARDS HELPED US KEEP HIM STABLE, BUT HE SAYS THAT WILLIE PULLING THROUGH WOULD BE A MIRACLE.
THAT IS EXACTLY WHAT I HAVE JUST PROVIDED.

ARE YOU SURE THIS IS A GOOD IDEA? MAKING SOMEONE IMMORTAL WITHOUT THEIR CONSENT SEEMS KINDA DODGY.
THE PRIORITY IS TO SAVE HIM. THIS WILL BUY HIM ENOUGH TIME TO HEAL, AND TIME FOR ME TO LEARN HOW TO REVERSE THE PROCESS. IDEALLY BEFORE HE WAKES AND WE HAVE SOME EXPLAINING TO DO.
HEY, YOU'RE STARTING TO SOUND LIKE ME!
THAT'S TROUBLING.

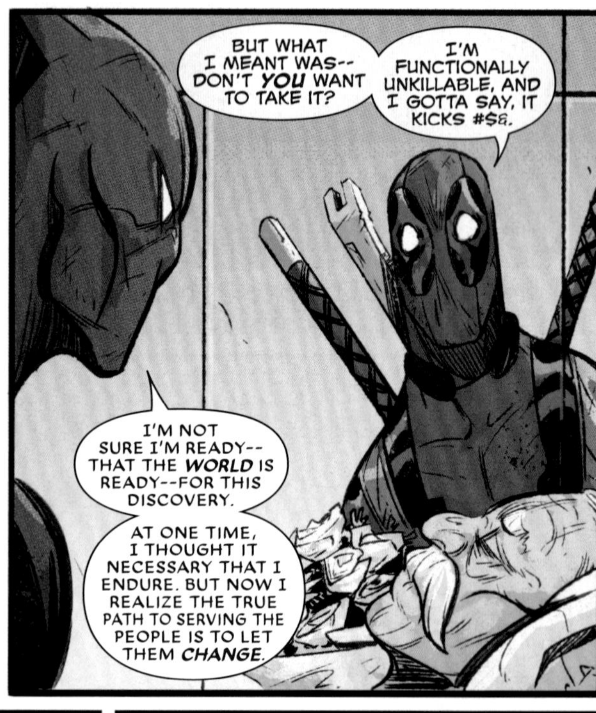
BUT WHAT I MEANT WAS-- DON'T YOU WANT TO TAKE IT?
I'M FUNCTIONALLY UNKILLABLE, AND I GOTTA SAY, IT KICKS #$&.
I'M NOT SURE I'M READY-- THAT THE WORLD IS READY--FOR THIS DISCOVERY.
AT ONE TIME, I THOUGHT IT NECESSARY THAT I ENDURE. BUT NOW I REALIZE THE TRUE PATH TO SERVING THE PEOPLE IS TO LET THEM CHANGE.

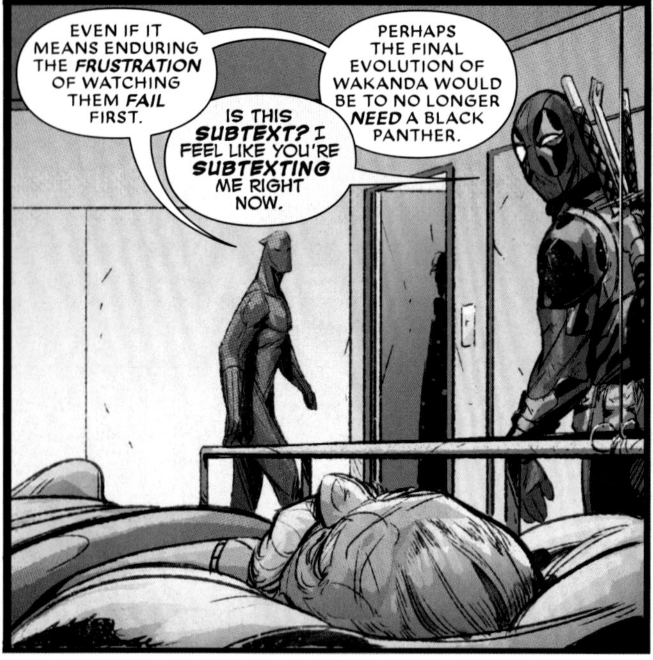
EVEN IF IT MEANS ENDURING THE FRUSTRATION OF WATCHING THEM FAIL FIRST.
PERHAPS THE FINAL EVOLUTION OF WAKANDA WOULD BE TO NO LONGER NEED A BLACK PANTHER.
IS THIS SUBTEXT? I FEEL LIKE YOU'RE SUBTEXTING ME RIGHT NOW.

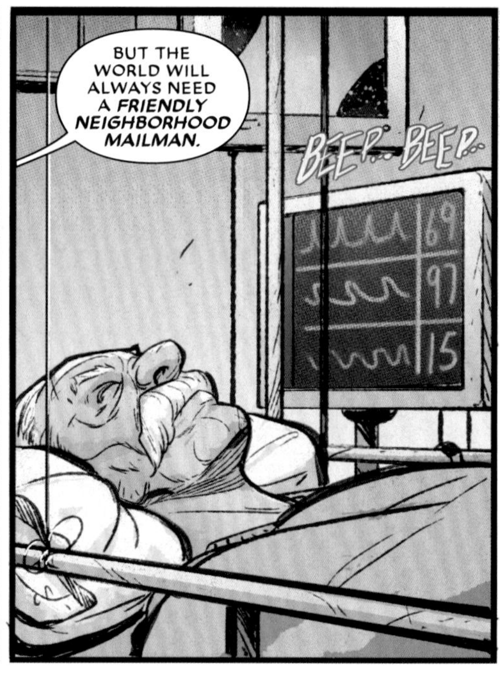
BUT THE WORLD WILL ALWAYS NEED A FRIENDLY NEIGHBORHOOD MAILMAN.
BEEP.. BEEP..
69
97
15

SHURI, I HAVE THE ITEMS. WILL YOU BE ABLE TO REVERSE ENGINEER THE TELEPORTATION FREQUENCY?
EITHER THAT OR ACCIDENTALLY TELEPORT THE ENTIRE STATE OF NEW JERSEY INTO THE VACUUM OF SPACE.
WORTH THE RISK.

FAREWELL, DEADPOOL. WE WILL NOT MEET AGAIN.
EH, I'D CHECK THE SALES FIGURES FIRST.
HEY, T'CHALLA. THAT STUFF I SAID BACK THERE. I KNOW I'LL NEVER BE AS PERFECT AS YOU.

NO ONE IS PERFECT, WADE. NOT ME, AND NOT YOU.
ESPECIALLY NOT YOU.
I KNOW. BUT I'M TRYING, YA KNOW? AND I JUST WANNA SAY... FROM THE BOTTOM OF MY HEART...

HOW DO THE AVENGERS DECORATE FOR A PARTY?

WITH AN EIGHT-FOOT BANNER! GET IT?
GOODBYE, WADE.
IF YOU LEAVE THAT MEANS YOU FORFEIT!

HEH. "EIGHT-FOOT BANNER."
DEADPOOL WINS!!!
END.
DEADPOOL WILL RETURN IN: DEADPOOL VS. FIN FANG FOOM!
WE'RE NOT DOING THAT, WADE. --WIL
IT'S GONNA BE AWESOME.

Adi Granov
1 VARIANT

Cully Hamner & Laura Martin
1 VARIANT

Steve Skroce & Dave Stewart
2 VARIANT

Ozgur Yildirim
3 VARIANT

Ricardo López Ortiz
4 VARIANT

Kyle Baker

5 VARIANT